Introduction to Educational Research

ISMAIL THAMARASSERI

KANISHKA PUBLISHERS, DISTRIBUTORS
NEW DELHI-110 002

KANISHKA PUBLISHERS, DISTRIBUTORS
4697/5-21A, Ansari Road, Daryaganj
New Delhi -110 002
Phones : 2327 0497, 2328 8285
Fax : 011-2328 8285
E-mail : kanishka_publishing@yahoo.co.in

Introduction to Educational Research
Edition-2014

PRINTED IN INDIA

Published by Madan Sachdeva for Kanishka Publishers, Distributors, 4697/5-21A, Ansari Road, Daryaganj, New Delhi-110 002, Typeset by Sunshine Graphics, Delhi, and Printed at Rajdhani Printers, Delhi.

Preface

Research methodology is taught as a supporting subject in several ways in many academic disciplines such as Psychology, Education, Sociology, Library and Information Science and Marketing Research etc.

This book is intended to serve as a text for courses in research methods in education, psychology and other social science subjects at the graduate and post graduate level. The book presented in simple language and easy to grasp style so that students may follow the subject matter easily. All professional students should be familiar with the methods of research and the analysis of data. They should also be able to use this information to interpret and critically analyze research reports and findings that appear in journals and other publications. Regarding the organization, the book consists 15 Chapters, well arranged in a coherent manner. It is hoped that the book shall provide guidelines to all interested research studies of one sort or the other.

This book couldn't have been written without contribution from a number of people, and I am indebted to each of them for their support and encouragement. I am indebted to the various authors, research scholars, and educationists whose views and opinions have been incorporated in the text, the names of which have been duly incorporated in the bibliographies given towards the end of the work. The author expresses his gratitude to the writers and publishers of these works. The author shall ever remain obliged to his teachers, parents, friends, family members, students, teacher trainees, colleagues for their directions and guidance. The author is also great thankful to M/s. Infratec Computer Systems, Calicut

University for the Computerization of the work. To them all, the author offers his greatful thanks to M/s. Kanishka Publishers, Distributors, New Delhi who came forward willingly to undertake the publishing of this book at a short time.

ISMAIL THAMARASSERI

Contents

Preface v

1. **Introduction to Educational Research** 1
   - Educational Research—Definitions
   - Research—Characteristics
   - The Functions of Research
   - Limitations of Educational Research

2. **Classification of Educational Research** 11
   - Types of Research
   - Basic Research
   - Need and Significance for Research in Education

3. **Applied and Evaluative Research** 17
   - Classification of Research by Purpose
   - Applied Research
     - Nature of Applied Research
     - Characteristics of Applied Research
   - Basic Versus Applied Research
   - Distinction Between Action Research and Applied Research
   - Evaluative Research
     - Nature of Evaluation Research
     - Evaluation—Is a Research

4. **Scientific Method and Its Use in Research** 30
   - Evolution of Science
   - The Scientific Method
   - Application of the Scientific Method in Education

5. **Action Research** 35

- Fundamental to Action Research
- Importance of Action Research
- Historical Background
- Value of Action Research in India
- Methodology of Action Research
- Scope and Advantages of Action Research
- Limitations of Action Research

6. **Case Study** 47

- Case Study – Meaning and Significance
- Characteristics of Case Study Method
- Steps of Case Study Method
- Uses of Case Study
- Limitations of Case Study

7. **Correlational Research** 53

- Types of Correlation
  - Positive and Negative Correlation
  - Linear and Non Linear Correlation
- Purpose of Correlational Research
- Basic Steps in Correlational Research
  - Sample
  - Instruments
  - Design and Procedures
  - Data Collection
  - Data Analysis and Interpretation

8. **Selection of Research Problem: Detection of Research Areas** 57

- The Research Problem
  - Knowing the Field
  - Selection of the Problem
- Detection of Research Areas
  - Professional Experience
  - Inference from Theory
  - Professional Literature
  - Technological and Social Changes
  - Discussions
  - Questioning Attitude
  - Consultations

- Questions One Need to Ask when Selecting a Problem
- Characteristics of a Good Research Problem

9. Sources of Information 67
- Internet
- Websites
- Search Engines
- E-mail

10. Selecting and Evaluating Problems; Statement of the Problem 70
- Selection of the Problem
- Criteria for Selecting and Evaluating Research Problem
- Statement of the Problem

11. Variables 80
- Types of Variables
  - Dependent and Independent Variables
  - Confounded Variables
    - ❖ Intervening Variables
    - ❖ Extraneous Variables
  - Qualitative and Categories Variables
    - ❖ Two Quantitative Variables
    - ❖ One Categorical and one Quantitative Variables
    - ❖ Two Categorical Variables
  - Continuous and Discrete Variables
  - Manipulated and Out Come Variables
    - ❖ Experimental Group
    - ❖ Control Group

12. Hypotheses 88
- Importance of the Hypotheses
- Formulation of Hypotheses
- Criteria of Usable Hypotheses
- Advantages and Disadvantages of Hypotheses
- Statement of Hypotheses

- Classification of Stating Hypotheses or Types of Hypotheses

13. **Sampling** 96
- Need for Sampling
- Some Important Definitions of Related Terms
- Bases of Sampling
- Characteristics of a Good Sample
- Use of Sampling
- Steps in Sampling Procedure
- Advantages and Disadvantages of Sampling
- Size of the Sample
- Representative Character of the Sample
- Reliability of the Sampling
- Selection of a Sample
- Different Methods of Sampling
- Probability and Non-Probability Sampling
- Various Classifications of Sampling Methods
- Errors in Sampling-Sampling Error

14. **Measures of Central Tendency** 124
- Computation of Arithmetic Mean
  - Calculation of Simple Arithmetic Mean
  - Calculation of Arithmetic Mean for Discrete Series
  - Mean-Merits and Demerits
- The Median
  - Calculation of Median for Discrete Series
  - Merits and Demerits of Median
- The Mode
  - Calculation of Mode for Individual Observations
  - Calculation of Mode for Discrete Scores with Frequencies
  - Mode-Merits and Demerits

15. **Research Proposal** 131
- Research Proposal/Synopsis/Plan for Research
- Types of Research Proposal
- Preparation of Research Proposal

– Introduction Part
– Procedual Part
– Bibliography
– Time Schedule
– Budget Schedule
– General Comments

Bibliography **140**
Index **146**

1

Introduction to Educational Research

Educational Research – Definitions

Educational Research is scientific and disciplined inquiry using quantitative and qualitative approaches. Educators and others use basic, applied and evaluation research for different purposes.

Research is a systematic process of collecting and logically analyzing data and information for some purpose.

Educational Research is not limited to the approaches used in the physical and natural sciences, nor should the word 'research' be used indiscriminately to describe what is actually casual observation and speculation.

Research is a systematic process of collecting and logically analyzing data for some purpose. Educational research is disciplined inquiry in which different disciplines provide different principles of research by which to collect and reason from data.

Research is a more systematic activity that is directed towards discovery and the development of an organized body of knowledge.

Research may be defined as the systematic and objective analysis and recording of controlled observations that may lead to the development of generalizations, principles or theories, resulting in prediction and possibly ultimate control of events.

"Research has come to be applied to such a wide range of activities within the field of education that it has ceased to have a single identifiable meaning."

—Robert, M.W.

"Research is a point of view, an attitude of inquiry of frame of mind. It asks questions which hither to not been asked, and it seeks to answer them by following a fairly definite procedure. It is not a mere theorizing, but rather an attempt to elicit facts and to face them once they have been assembled."

– Rusk (Research – A Point of View—An Attitude of Inquiry)

"The systematic and scholarly applications of the scientific method, interpreted in its broader sense to the solution of educational problems; conversely, an systematic study designed to promote the development of education as a science can be considered educational research."

– George G. Mouly

'Research a systematic and scholarly application of the scientific method'. "To be sure, the best research is that which is reliable, verifiable and exhaustive, so that it it provides information in which we have confidence."

– Francis G. Cornell

'Research – An Information in which we have confidence' –

"Research is essentially a stake of mind—a friendly, welcoming attitude towards change."

– Madhuri Singh (Research A Stake of Mind)

"Research is a careful inquiry of examination in seeking facts or principles, a diligent investigation to ascertain something."

– Clifford Woody (Research a Careful Inquiry)

"Research is simply a systematic and refined technique of thinking, employing specialized tools, instruments and procedures in order to obtain a more adequate solution of a problem than would possible under ordinary means."

– C.C. Crawford

"Research is considered to be the more formal, systematic, intensive process of carrying on the scientific method of analysis. It involves a more systematic structure of investigation, usually resulting in some sort of formal record of produce and a report of results or conclusions."

– Best

"Research, Ideally is the careful unbiased investigation of a problem based in so far as possible upon demonstrable facts and involving refined distinctions, interpretations and usually some generalizations."

– E. Wayne

"Educational research is that activity which is directed towards development of a science of behaviour in educational situations. The ultimate aim of such a science is to provide knowledge that will permit the educator to achieve his goals by the most effect methods."

– Travers

Research – Characteristics

Research may be defined as the systematic and objective analysis and recording of controlled observations that may lead to the development of generalizations, principles or theories resulting in prediction and possibly ultimate control of events.

Because definitions of this sort are rather abstract, a summary of some of the characteristics may help to clarify its spirit and meaning.

1. Research is directed toward the solution of a problem. The ultimate goal is to discover cause and effect relationships between variables through researchers often have to settle for the useful discovery of systematic relationships because the evidence for a cause and effect relationship is insufficient.

2. Research-emphasis the development of generalizations, principles of theories that will be helpful in predicting future occurrences. Research usually goes beyond the specific objects, groups or situations investigated and infers characteristics of a target population from the sample observed. Research is more than information retrieval, the simple gathering of information. Although many school research departments gather and tabulate statistical information that may be useful in decision making. These activities are not properly learned research.

3. Research is based upon observable experience or empirical evidence. Certain interesting questions do not lend themselves to research procedures because they cannot be observed. Research rejects revelation and dogma as methods of establishing knowledge and accepts only what can be verified by observation.

4. Research demands accurate observation and description. Research use quantitative measuring devices, the most precise form of description. When this is not possible or appropriate, they use qualitative or non-qualitative description of their observation. They select or devise valid data-gathering procedures and, when feasible, employ mechanical, electronic, or psychometric devices to retire, observation, description, and analysis of data.

5. Research involves gathering new data from primary or first hand sources or using existing data for a new purpose. Teachers frequently assign a so-called research project that involves writing a paper dealing with the life of a prominent person. The students are expected to react a number of encyclopedias, books or periodicals, and to synthesize the information in a written report. This is not research, for the data are not new. Merely re-organizing or restating what is already known and has already been written, valuable

as if may be as a learning experience, is not research. It adds, nothing to what is known.

6. Although research activity many at times be some what random and unsystematic, it is more often characterized by carefully designed procedures that apply rigorous analysis. Although trial and error are often involved research is rarely a blind, shot gun investigation or an experiment just to see what happens.

7. Research requires expertise. The researcher known what is already known but the problem and how others have investigated it. He or she has reached the related literature carefully and is also thoroughly grounded in the terminology, concepts and technical skills necessary to understand and analyze the data gathered.

Scope of Educational Research

The scope of educational research is very vast. Educational research has made considerable gains in knowledge. Some educational research, especially the measurement of intelligence and achievement, has a long tradition of solving methodological problems. Our society and educational leaders have used research increasingly to aid in policy—and decision making.

The Functions of Research

Fundamental/Basic/Pure Research

Basic research has drawn its pattern and spirit from the physical sciences and has represented a rigorous, structured type of analysis. We have presented the goal of research as the development of theories by the discovery of broad generalizations or principles. We have employed careful sampling procedures in order to extend the findings beyond the group or situation studied. So far our discussions has shown little concern for the application of the findings to actual problems in areas considered to be the concern of people other than the investigator. This methodology is the approach of basic or fundamental research.

Fundamental research is usually carried on in a laboratory situation, sometimes with animals as subjects. This type of research has been primarily the activity of psychologists rather than educators.

Action Research

Action Research is focused on immediate application, not on the development of theory or an general application. It has placed its emphasis on a problem here and now in a local setting. Its findings are to be evaluated in terms of local applicability, not universal validity. Its purpose is to improve school, practices and at the same time, to improve those who try to improve the practices to continue research processes habits of thinking, ability to work harmoniously with others, and professional spirit.

Assessment Research

Assessment is a fact finding activity that describes conditions that exist at a particular time. No hypothesis are proposed or tested, no variable relationships are examined, and no recommendations for action are suggested.

Descriptive Research

Descriptive research unlike assessment evaluation and concerned with all of the following: hypothesis formulation and testing, the analysis of the relationships between non-manipulated variables and the development of generalization.

Limitations of Educational Research

Knowledge acquired through research is limited by the nature of both educational practice and research. Educational research is constrained by ethical and legal considerations in conducting research on human beings, the public nature of education, the complexity of educational practices, and methodological limitations. Each of these four constraints ultimately influences our knowledge about education.

1. *Human Subjects:* Educational research focuses primarily on human beings. The researcher is ethically responsible

for protecting the rights and welfare of the subjects. While conducting a study researchers must protect subjects from physical and mental discomfort, harm and danger. Many studies require informal consent from the subjects, parents or institution, and there are laws no protect, the confidentiality of the data and the privacy of the individual. Researcher have followed many of these ethical principles informally for years. These principles informally for years. These principles often impose limitations on the kinds of studies that can be conducted in valid and objective ways in education. Physical and mental discomfort of subject may affect the length of testing periods, the replication of studies, the types of treatments and ultimately the research questions investigated.

2. *Public Institution:* Education is a public enterprise influence by the external environment. Although many practices seem to undergo no drastic change, the institution change. An elementary school can change its entire faculty and school population every seven years. The community surrounding a school can change drastically when industry or an ethnic group establishes itself in this area. Legislative mandates and judicial orders have changed the structure of schools and added or delected programmes. Because schools exist for educational purposes, not for research purposes, studies cannot unduly interfere with educational processes. Longitudinal and replication studies on a changing elientele and institution are difficult to conduct. It is often said that we do not know ultimately the effects of schooling because these effects may occur years later outside an educational setting.

3. *Complexity of Research Problems:* A third facts that limits educational research is the complexity of the research problems. The human beings involved in complex living organisms, and they actively select the environmental stimuli, to which they respond. Different individuals possess the stimuli differently. Educational research

has demonstrated the complexities of individual differences and that responses to stimuli may be predictable and unpredictable. The educational researcher thus deals simultaneously with many variables often ambiguous ones in a single study. In addition, there is a growing awareness among social scientists that individuals cannot be studied meaningfully outside the context of real life. Behaviour is determined by both individual and situational characteristics, and to study individuals without regard to situations is incomplete. Thus, educational researchers not only must content with individual differences among people, they must also consider a myriad of situational elements.

4. *Methodological Difficulties:* A fourth factor that limits quantitative educational research is methodological difficulties. Educational research measures complex human characteristics, thinking and problem solving skills. The measurement of achievement, intelligence, leadership styles, group interaction or readiness skills involves conceptual definitions and issues of validity and reliability. Some educational research has been possible only as valid and reliable instruments were developed. Other research has been delayed by a lack of valid instruments.

   Qualitative research also has methodological difficulties, especially those inherent in the researchers decisions involving which data collection and data analysis methods to use to assure valid findings. Qualitative research is sometimes criticized from conventional view point for the lack of reliable and generalizable findings and the tendency to focus on the unique elements of education rather than the common elements.

5. *Difficulties in Observation*: Observation of human behaviour is more subjective than the observation of physical or biological phenomena. The subjectivity on

the part of the observer has a direct impact on the interpretation and findings on which he bases his conclusions.

6. *Difficulties in Replication:* The physicist can find objectively and accurately resistance of a wire in the laboratory. He can report his findings and the experiment can be easily replicated by others. This is not easily possible in Education. A teacher in India may not be able to reproduce the conditions of an American teacher's experimental teaching method with the same precision of replication as that with which an Indian physicist can reproduce an American physicist's experiment. Educational phenomena are singular events and can hardly be replicated for the purposes of observation with the same degree of precision and objectivity.

7. *Interaction of Observer and Subjects:* The researcher in the field of education is also human being. His presence as an observer in a situation may change the behaviour of his human subjects. For example, the school children may not exhibit their natural behaviour when they know that they are being observed for a particular type of behaviour.

8. *Difficulties in Control:* The rigid control of experimental conditions is possible in the laboratory of physical or biological sciences. It is not possible in educational studies in which the researcher has to deal with the human subjects and many variables simultaneously.

9. *Measurement Problems:* The tools used for measurement and data collection in the educational studies are much less valid and reliable than the tools of the natural scientists.

REFERENCES

1. Best, J.W. (1951). *Research in Education*, New Delhi: Prentice Hall.
2. Good, C.V. *et. al.*, (1951). *Methodology of Educational Research*, New York: Prentice Hall.
3. Sukhia, S.P. *et. al.*, (1966). *Elements of Educational Research*. New Delhi: Allied Publishers.
4. Traver, R.M.V.S. (1964). *An Introduction to Educational Research*. New Delhi: McGraw Hill.

2
Classification of Educational Research

Types of Research/Classification of Research

Research is classified on the basis of the objectives or the purposes the researcher intends to accomplish. Generally research is classified into three,

1. Fundamental/Pure/Basic Research.
2. Applied Research.
3. Action Research.

Basic Research

Research is basic when it is not concerned with day to day phenomena and problems. It is rather concerned with the solution of fundamental problems and major or vital issues. According to Travers, "Basic research is designed to add to an organized body of scientific knowledge and does not necessarily produce result of immediate practical value" (1948). Kerlings, "Basic Research is research done to test theory... while little or no thought of applications of the results of the research to practical problems" (1979).

Basic research is concerned exclusively with knowing, explaining and predicting rational and social phenomena. It deals with a theory, a basic principles or a generalization. Its major aim is to obtain and use the empirical data to formulate, expand and evaluate theory. Such an approach often leads to knowledge for knowledge's sake.

Basic research draws its pattern and spirit from the physical sciences. It represents a rigorous and structured type analysis. If employs careful sampling procedures in order to extend the findings beyond the group or situation and thus develops theories by discovering proved generalizations or principles. It is usually carried on in an laboratory or other sterile environment, sometimes with animals. This type of research, which has no immediate or planned application, may later result in further research of an applied nature.

Abstractness, another important aspect of science, is important to any thereby in basic research. It has never been designed for solving human and social problem, making decisions and taking action. The scientist is pre occupied with developing knowledge and is not expected nor required to spell out the practical implications of a study. To do this requires a leap from an abstract. Level of discourse to a concrete and specific land.

The effects of basic research are felt indirectly only over considerable periods of time because new knowledge challenges fixed sets of beliefs and dogma studies conducted by Piaget and his collegues in the cognitive development of children have created impact only later. Basic research influences indirectly the ways people think and perceive, as impact that may or may not lead to action.

Thus the purpose of basic research is first to add to our knowledge of basic principles and scientific laws. Second basic research advances scientific inquiry and methodology and indirectly the methodology of applied research. Basic research may have a more overt influence on applied research by identifying theories to be tested in a field of application such as medicine or education.

Using basic research methodology, researchers may test theories of learning cognitive development, creativity and others in instructional programmes. Basic research methodologies, especially measurement and evaluation are used on adapted to applied and action researcher.

Table–2.1
Functions of Types of Research

Basic Research	*Applied Research*
Topic of Research	*Applied Field*
Physical, Behavioural and Social Sciences.	Medicine, Education, Engineering.
Level of Discourage/Generalizability – Abstract, related to science.	General, related to a given field.
Purpose	
1. Tests, theories, scientific laws, basic principle.	1. Tests the usefulness of scientific theories within a given field.
2. Determine empirical relationships among phenomena and analytical generalizations.	2. Determine empirical relationships and analytical generalizations within a given field.
Intended Use	
1. Add to scientific knowledge of basic laws and principle.	1. Add to research based knowledge in a given field.
2. Advance further inquiry and methodology.	2. Advance research and methodology in a given field.

Table–2.2
Comparison of Fundamental Research and Action Research with Regard to Different Aspects

Aspects	*Fundamental Research*	*Action Research*
Objectives	Its purpose is to develop and test educational theories and to obtain universally applicable principles.	Knowledge obtained is intended to be applied in local setting. It also provides a sort of Inservice training to participating field workers.
Expertise	Expert training is needed in measurement, research methodology and statistics.	Only a ordinary training is required. It can be done began average teacher under the guidance of a consultant.

Contd...

Aspects	*Fundamental Research*	*Action Research*
Involvement	The research works may not be personally involved in the problem he selects for research.	The teacher is invariably involved in the research problem.
Locating the research problem	A wide range of methods and a vast process is used to locate the research problem.	It deals with the problems which hinder classroom teaching learning process. Thus the participating teachers can easily identify them.
Hypothesis	Highly specific and well stated hypothesis are formulated and adopted.	Only the specific statement of the problem serves as a hypothesis.
Review of literature	It necessitates on exhaustive and thorough review of literature in order to have a complete understanding of the accumulated knowledge in the area.	It depends simply a general understanding of the area. There is no need for a thorough and intensive review.
Sampling	A random or otherwise unbiased sample of the population is studied.	Pupils studying in the particular class taught by the teacher are used as subjects.
Design	Careful attention is paid to maintain comparable conditions thus reducing error and bias.	Procedures are planned only in general terms.
Analysis of Data	Complex analysis is often called for.	Simple procedures for analysis are sufficient.
Statistical treatment	There is stress on belittling statistical treatment of data for the sake of objectivity.	Not much stress on objectivity and statistical treatment. Even the subjective opinion of participating teacher is given weightage.
Application of results	The research findings usually remain confined to research reports and publications. There is no co-ordination between the research workers and field workers and field workers to ensure utilization of valuable conclusions.	Findings are applied straight way to the classes of participating teachers and lead to for reaching improvements in the teaching learning process.

We can see that research in it different forms—fundamental, applied, action-is an. Inevitable step in the process of education. Research is not an end, but the means to an end. Research develops new theories, modifies existing theories, applies theories in specific fields or brings immediately in two classroom practice the research findings. So from our analysis we can easily that research is one of the major areas of study which brings education closer to 'science'.

Need and Significance for Research in Education

1. Research economizes effort and increases efficiency.
2. Research dignifies the work of the teacher.
3. Research brings confidence to the teacher.
4. Research leads to the adoption of new methods.
5. Research brings a sense of awareness.
6. Research keeps us alert.
7. Better understanding of the teaching-learning process.
8. Research as controlling factor of social behaviour.
9. Research promotes educational reform.
10. Research brings objectivity.
11. Research leads to cultural and social and scientific development.
12. Research needed for selection.
13. Educational Research for Identifying talent.

The significance of each letter of the word 'RESEARCH' may be seen as,

R—Rational way of thinking
E—Expert and Exhaustive Treatment
S—Search for solutions
E—Exactness

A – Analysis of Adequate Data
R – Relationship of facts

C – *(a)* Caseful recording
(b) Critical observation
(c) Constructive attitude
(d) Condensed and compactly stated – generalizations

H – Honesty and Hardwork in all aspects of the treatment of data.

REFERENCES

1. Good, C.V. *et. al.,* (1951). *Methodology of Educational Research,* New York: Prentice Hall.
2. Mc Burney, Donal, H. (2001). Research Methods Australia: Wordsworth.
3. Mouly, G.J. (1964). *The Science of Educational Research.* New Delhi: McGraw Hill.
4. Traver, R.M.V.S. (1964). *An Introduction to Educational Research.* New Delhi: McGraw Hill.

3

Applied and Evaluative Research

Introduction

Research is a more systematic activity that is directed toward discovery and the development of an organized body of knowledge. Research is a careful inquiry of examination in seeking facts or principles; a diligent investigation to ascertain something (*Clifford Woody, 'Research a Careful Inquiry'*).

Educational Research is scientific and disciplined inquiry using quantitative and qualitative approaches. Educators and others use basic, applied and evaluative research for different purposes.

Classification of Research by Purpose

Classification of Research by purpose is based primarily on the degree which findings have direct educational application and the degree to which they are generalizable to other educational situations. Both of these criteria are a function of the research control exercised during the conduction of the study.

Basic research involves the development of theory; Applied research is concerned with application of theory to the solution of problems; Evaluation research involves decision making regarding the relative worth of two or more alternative actions; Research and Development is directed at the development of effective products that can be used in the schools; and action research is concerned with immediate solution to local problems.

Applied Research

Applied research in a field of common practice and is concerned with the application and development of research-based knowledge about that practice; medicine, engineering, social work and education are applied field that use scientific knowledge but are not themselves science. "Applied research (as opposed to basic research) is aimed at producing knowledge relevant to providing a solution (generalizable) to a general problem". (*Worthers and Sanders*, 1973, p. 23). In other words, applied research/studies focus an research problems common to a given field.

Applied research tests the usefulness of scientific theories and determines empirical and analytical relationships within a given field.

For example, a scientists, might investigate and try to understand human intelligence in its many manifestations, including schooling. An Educational research might determine the relationship of intelligence to achievement or analyze court rulings on the instructional use of certain books. Implications of such studies are stated in general terms and not us specific recommendations for immediate action.

Applied research, like basic research, is abstract and general, using the language common to those in the field. Many educational studies on achievement, teaching, learning, excemptional children and the like use terms that have a special meaning within the profession. The generalizability of applied research is usually limited to the delineated field. Educational research thus focuses on knowledge about educational theories and practices rather than an universal knowledge.

Education as an applied field of common practices, it is not yet recognized as a science. Similar to the established social sciences and disciplines, the generalization and verification of theories to develop scientific knowledge about education is highly valued. In early periods of developing a discipline from an applied field, however initial efforts are usually directed more towards establishing empirical facts. In later periods, facts from separate studies can be synthesized and ultimately integrated into theories.

Educational research in general, has focused on establishing empirical facts and frameworks (*Clifford*, 1973). The development of new research methodologies, especially research synthesis may enable researches to identify those educational theoretical frameworks which have substantial empirical evidence (*Walberg*, 1986).

Applied research adds to the research based knowledge in the given field. The efforts of applied research are felt in directly over a period of time. When a series of studies are presented, published and critiqued for an considerable time, this knowledge influences the way practitioners think and perceive a common problem. Applied research stimulates further research and suggest new theories of practice and science and can stimulate basic research and methodological development. An example is the development of more appropriate statistics to study phenomena that relate to school achievement (*Kerlinger*, 1979). The need to measure learning at different ages has stimulated basic research. In the measurement of child and adult intelligence.

Nature of Applied Research

Applied research is directed towards the solution of immediate, specific and practical problems. It is performed in relation to actual problems and under the conditions in which they are found in practice. The Goal of applied research in terms of adding scientific knowledge acquires only a secondary position. It places importance on a problem here and now.

Applied research also uses the scientific method of inquiry. It has most of the characteristics of basic research. More over its findings are to be evaluated in terms of universal validity. Applied research is mainly intended to improve school practices and add to greater teacher effectiveness in a practical manner. Most of the problems faced by teachers, policy planners and administers are solved through applied researches.

Characteristics of Applied Research

Applied research has most of the characteristics of fundamental research, including the use of sampling techniques and the subsequent inferences about the target population. However, its purpose is improving a product or a process-testing theoretical concepts in actual problem situations. Most educational research is applied research, for its attempts to develop generalizations about teaching-learning processes and instructional materials.

Applied research though in no way less rigorous in the approach, focuses its attention on certain issues from the beginning. An example is modern research into learning theory, which while extending general knowledge has, as one of its objectives, the application of its findings to a number of areas.

The point is that, applied research seeks generalizations from a large number cases and that the link between the research finding and their application need not be immediate.

Another feature of applied research is that the link between those who do the research and those who apply it need not normally be a close one. The dissemination of information is often second-hand via books, articles and teaching.

Basic Versus Applied Research

It is difficult to discuss basic and applied research separately, as they are really on a continuum. Classification of a given study along this continuum is based primarily on the degree to which they are generalizable to other educational situations. Both of these criteria are a function of the research control exercised during the execution of the study. Basic research, either directly or indirectly, involves the development of theory; applied research is concerned with the application of theory to the solution of problems.

There is disagreement among educators and researches concerning toward which end of the basic-applied continuum research should be directed. In its purest form, basic research is conducted solely for the purpose of theory development and refinement. It is not concerned with practical applicability and most closely resembles the laboratory conditions and controls usually associated with scientific research. Applied research, as the name implies, is conducted for the purpose of applying, or testing, theory and evaluating its usefulness in solving educational problems. Rightly or wrongly, most educational research studies would be classified at the applied end of the continuum; they are more concerned with "What" works best than with "Why". Basic research is concerned with establishing general principles of learning; applied research is concerned with their utility in educational settings. For example, much basic research has been conducted with animals to determine principles of reinforcement and their effect on learning. Applied research has tested these principles to determine their effectiveness in improving learning. (For example, Programmed micro computer instruction) and behaviour (For example behaviour modification). Some studies, those located in the middle of the continuum, try to integrate both approaches by conducting controlled research in special or simulated classrooms, using school children, and involving school-relevant topics and materials. Both types of research are necessary. Basic research provides the theory that produces the implications for solving educational problem; applied research provides data to support theory, guide theory revision, or suggest development of new theory.

At the "most" applied end of the continuum there are several kinds of research worthy of special note: evaluation research, research and development (R&D), and action research. Evaluation research involves decision making regarding the relative worth of two or more alternative decisions; research and development is directed at the development of products that can be used in the schools; and the action research is concerned with immediate solutions to real problems.

Table–3.1
Basic Versus Applied Research

Basic Research	*Applied Research*
Either directly on indirectly involves the development of theory.	Applied research is concerned with the application of theory to the solution of problems.
Is conducted solely for the purpose of theory development and refinement.	It is not concerned with practical applicability and most closely resembles the laboratory conditions and controls usually associated with scientific research.
Is concerned with establishing general principles of learning.	Is concerned with their utility in educational settings.
It provides the theory that produces the implications for solving educational problem.	It provides data to support theory, guide theory revision or suggest development of new theory.

Table–3.2
Distinction Between Action Research and Applied Research

Action Research	*Applied Research*
Action research interprets the scientific method much more loosely, chiefly because its focus is a specific problem in a specific setting.	Applied research is concerned mainly with establishing relationship and testing theories, it is quite rigorous in its application of the conditions of this method.
Projects become more extensive in their coverage.	The conditions imposed on applied research are normally relaxed with action research.

Distinction Between Action Research and Applied Research

Applied research and Action research are similar in some ways, there are important differences between them which need to be made explicit, for confusion between the two does sometimes arise. Both utilize the scientific method.

Table–3.3
Functions of Types of Research

Basic Research	*Applied Research*
Topic of Research	*Applied Field*
Physical, behavioural and social sciences.	Medicine, education, engineering etc.
Levels of discourse/generalizability	
Abstract, related to science.	General; related to a given field.
Purpose	
1. Tests theory, scientific laws, basic principles.	1. Tests the usefulness of scientific theories within given field.
2. Determine empirical relationships among phenomena and analytical generalizations.	2. Determine empirical relationships and analytical generalizations within a given field.
Intended Use	
1. Add to scientific knowledge of basic law and principles.	1. Add to research based knowledge in a given field.
2. Advance further inquiry and methodology.	2. Advance research and methodology in a given field.

Since applied research is concerned mainly with establishing relationships and testing theories, it is quite rigorous in its application of the conditions of this method. To this end, therefore it insists on: studying a large number of cases; establishing as much control as possible over variables; precise sampling techniques; and a serious concern to generalize its findings to comparable situations. It does not claim to contribute directly to the solution of problems.

Action Research, by contrast, interprets the scientific method much more loosely, chiefly because its focus is a specific problem in a specific setting. The emphasis is not so much on obtaining generalizable scientific knowledge as on precise knowledge for a particular situation and purpose. The conditions imposed on applied research, therefore, are normally relaxed with action research. Ofcourse, as action research projects become more extensive in their coverage, the boundary between the two methods become less easy to define.

A curriculum projects involving 100 schools, say, or a community action programme embracing a number of major sub urban areas, will tend to yield rather more generalizable knowledge and information than purely localized undertakings.

Action research might be described as inquiry conducted in to a particular issue of current concern, usually undertaken by those directly involved, with the aim of implementing a change in a specific situation. Cohan and Manion have drawn out the distinctions between action research and applied research by suggesting that the conditions which usually govern applied research are some what more relaxed in action research. Since the latter focuses upon a specific situation or problem in specific setting (*Cohen and Manion*, 1986: 209).

Some people are inclined to differentiate action research from applied research in as much as former has relevance only to classroom situations, while the latter can probe in to practical problems of greater complexity and wider applicability.

Action Research According to Corey (1953, p. 145) is the research undertaken by practitioners so that they may improve their practices. Lehman and Manion (1971, p. 6) point out that; "Action research is type of applied or decision oriented research, but with the stipulation that the researcher is the same person as the practitioner who will make live with the decision."

Evaluative Research

'Evaluation', the systematic study of a particular programme or set of events over a period of time in order to asses effectiveness.

This research can be a case of simple appraisal carried out by an individual teacher into an aspect of curriculum or a nationally conducted survey such as that currently being undertaken by the National Foundation for Education Research into the Technical and Vocational Education Initiative (TVEI). The emphasis in evaluation is with the assessment of the effectiveness of particular programme or how well it has worked in terms of its aims.

Evaluation is concerned with the application of its findings and implies some judgement of the effectiveness, social utility, or desirability of a product, process or programme in terms of carefully defined and agreed upon objectives or values. It may involve recommendations for action. It is not concerned with generalization that may be extended to other settings. In education, it may seek ensures to such questions as: How well is the science programme developing the competencies that have been agreed upon by the faculty curriculum committee? Should the programme in vocational agriculture education be dropped? Are the library facilities adequate? Should the reading textbook series currently in use be retained?

Nature of Evaluation Research

Evaluation Research focuses on a particular practice at a given site(s). The practice may be a programme, a product or a process, but he crucial—Evaluation Research assess the merit and worth of a particular practice in terms of the values operating at the site(s). Evaluation determines whether the practice works—that is, does it do what is intended as the site?—Evaluation also determines whether the practice is worth the costs of development, implementation or wide spread adoption. Costs may be those of materials, time and space, staff skills and morale, and community concerns.

Formal evaluation can be conducted by researcher in a given field or by a practitioner at the site. Evaluation Research, which is as other types of research, generally required specialized training in several methodologies and disciplines as well as skills in interpersonal relations and communication. Many comprehensive evaluations contain both qualitative and quantitative data from a series of studies conducted at different implementation phases of the practice.

An evaluation study is communicated in concrete language which is specific to the practice and meaningful to the participant. The findings should have "site scientific interpretability" (*Campbell,* 1982). Because evaluation aids in immediate decision making, the findings should have limited generalizability. An innovative ecology curriculum in public schools, including the materials, staff and students will probably not survive the decade and is of little interest to schools with other environmental problems and instructional resources. Both applied and evaluation research may study practices common to many education settings, but the evaluation focuses first on the implementation of at a given site.

Evaluation research can add to our knowledge about a specific practice and can stimulate further research and methodological development to study practices.

Evaluation studies often identify variables or suggest hypothesis for other evaluation or suggest hypothesis for other evaluation and applied research. Qualitative holistic analysis of the sites context has emphasized the importance of certain methodologies. Assessment of achievement has encouraged measurement in education that was not attempt previously, such as the attributes of pupils aged to five years and excemptional children with special needs. A series of evaluation studies on the particular practice of diverse sites, such as Head start classrooms, or up on organization change processes. (*Rosenblum and Louis,* 1981) can add to the existing knowledge in the applied field.

Evaluation is the systematic process of collecting and analyzing data in order to make decisions. Evaluation involves questions such as the following:

1. Is this special programme worth what it costs?
2. Is the new experimental reading curriculum better than former curriculum?

3. Should Fenster be placed in a programme for the gifted?

Answers to these questions require the collection and analysis of data and interpretation of that data with respect to one or more criteria. While generally the more objective the criteria and data the better, some degree of subjectivity is unavoidable since how people *feel* is often an important variable. For example, whether a new experimental curriculum is "better" depends on the criteria for success. One obvious criterion would be student achievement. Other criteria might include student attitudes and teacher attitudes. Examination of test scores might reveal that students averaged two points higher with the new curriculum. Objectively, and strictly speaking, the new curriculum was "better" with represent to student achievement. School administers, however may have decide that an achievement difference of at least 10 points would be necessary in order to justify the time, effort and cost required to change over to the new curriculum. Further, teachers may have expressed the opinion that the new curriculum is burdensome, overly restrictive, and does not allow for any creativity in teaching.

Similarly, determining whether Fenster meets the criteria for admittance to the programme for the gifted (For example has a specific IQ score and grade point average) would be an objective process; setting the criteria themselves would be more subjective, as would teacher input.

Deciding whether a special programme is "worth" what it costs is even more complex and typically involves serious value judgement. If a special programme cost a school system Rs. 100,000 per school year but reduced school vandalism by the amount of Rs. 150,000, there would not be much disagreement concerning whether the programme was worth what it cost. But what if a programme cost Rs. 100,000 per school year and reduced the ninth-grade dropout rate by 5 per cent? How much is an education worth? How much is it worth to have a child increasing his or her knowledge instead of roaming the streets or attempting to enter an already crowded job market? Opinion on this issue varies greatly. The philosophy of the current school board would probably determine whether or not the programme continued.

Notice that in none of the examples was the purpose of the evaluation to determine whether something was "good", or worth while, as opposed to "bad", or 'worthless', per se. That is not the function of evaluation.

The purpose of evaluation is to select an alternative in order to make a decision. They may be only two alternatives (For example; Continue the programme or not, adopt the new curriculum or keep the current one) or there may be several alternatives (For example many textbooks may be available for adoption).

Evaluation—Is a Research?

A major point of disagreement among researchers is the issue of whether evaluation is a type of research or a separate desciple? A related issue is whether evaluations should be based on research designs, particularly when a group comparisons are involved such as; Does curriculum 'A' lead to higher achievement than curriculum 'B'? Some argue that educational research and educational evaluation have distinctly different purposes, that research seeks control while evaluation assess what is, and that the natural settings characteristic of evaluation essentially preclude that control. In reality, however, there is a fine line between research and evaluation, and an evaluation may very easily utilizes a research design. Both research and evaluation involve decision making and both involve steps which parallel those of the scientific method. Further many research studies are conducted in natural, real world settings and are subject to the same control problems involved in many evaluations. Thus, while the issue has not yet been resolved, the case seems stronger for classifying evaluation as a type of research whose purpose is to facilitate decision making.

Conclusion

Applied, basic and evaluation research differ primarily because of different purposes, functions and questions of investigation.

Basic research, which tests theories and explain empirical and analytical relations in the physical, behavioural and social sciences is used to establish scientific laws.

Applied research tests the usefulness of scientific theories in field of application and investigates practical relationship common to the given field. Neither basic nor applied research is designed to produce direct solution to a specific problem at a given site. After a considerable period of time, both types of research can influence indirectly the way scientists, researchers and practitioners think about the perceive their respective problems.

Evaluation research assesses the merit and worth of a particular practice of a give site(s) against one or more scales of values. Unlike basic and applied research, evaluation provides information for immediate use as a practice is developed, implemented and institutionalized.

REFERENCES

1. McMillan, J.H. and Sally Schumacher, S. (1989). *"Research in Education – A Conceptual Introduction"*: Second Edition. USA: Harper Collins Publishers.
2. Gay, L.R. (1996). *"Educational Research, Competencies for Analysis and Applications"*. UK: Prentice Hall Inc.
3. Hitchcock, G. and Hughes, D. (1989). *Research and the Teacher – A Qualitative Introduction to School Based Research"*. USA: Routledge Chapman and Hall Inc.
4. Diwan, R. (2002). *'Improving Quality of Educational Research'* Vol.1, 2. New Delhi. Atlantic Publication.
5. Sprinthall, R.C. *et. al.*, (1991). *"Understanding Educational Research"*. USA: Prentice Hall Inc.
6. Koul, L. (1997). *"Methodology of Educational Research"*. New Delhi: Vikash Publishing House (P) Ltd.
7. Cohen, L. and Manion, L. (1994). *"Research Methods in Education"* 4th Ed. New York, Routledge Publishers.

4

Scientific Method and Its Use in Research

Evolution of Science

"In the beginning God created the heaven and the earth." It was the beginning whether a person chooses to believe in religious or the scientific origin of life, there must be agreement that somewhere, somehow, it all began. It is form this beginning that everything has evolved. So it is with science and scientific method.

In the earliest stages of man's development, mythology was used almost entirely to explain unusual occurrences of everyday life which would, otherwise have remained a mystery forever. Using myths may seem a very crude manner of explanation to interpret the action of certain phenomena, compared to present day thinking, but it was a significant advance from that period in history when no explanation of any kind were given man had thus progressed from a non thinking animal to one who questioned existence of things around him.

Thus step by step using our imagination we can utilize the evaluation of science through out pre-historic times. The division of science into manageable parts had its beginning with Aristotle (384-322, BC). "Aristotle divided reality into several spheres of physics, biology, ethics, politics and psychology; and the reality which he studied in these spheres was the observable facts'.

Inductive Reasoning was also advanced by Aristotle. He believed in observing all things, classifying them precisely and form this arriving at generalizations.

Euclid (300 BC) at the science time added to the existing domain of science with his theories of geometry, derived from his method of reasoning, the deductive method.

The birth of present day science could be traced to Leonardo da Vinci' (1452-1519) Nicholas Copernicus (1473-1553), Vesalius (1514-1584) and Galileo Galilei (1564-1642) in the period of history known as the Renaissance. Sir Isacc Newton's (1642-1727) discovery enabled the accumulation of knowledge to finally result in a major break through the barrier of the unknown. Liovoister (1743-1794) in the field of chemistry, Charles Darvin (1809-1882)—genetics and heredity, Lowes Pasteur (1822-1895)—Bacteriology, Benjamin Franklin, Thomas Jefferson, Robert-Fulton, Thomas Edison, Alexander Gracham Bell, Albert Einstein *et. al.*, are made major contributions.

Today rapid strides are being made in all fields of science. This advance is being accomplished not in science but in the method. This scientific method is acquired through the correct use of methods of thought handed down by the scientists and which collectively is called the scientific method.

The Scientific Method

Francis Bacon (1561-1626) gave his theory of induction, Rene Descaretes (1596-1650) his ideal method, the theory of deduction, Moris Cohen (1880-1947), his method hypothesis come first, and John Dewey (1879-1952) the concept identification of the problem.

The scientific method may be defined as: "A collective term denoting the various processes by the aid of which the sciences are built up."

Scientific method consisting 4 major parts.

1. Identification of the problem.

2. Formulation of an hypothesis.
3. Systematically collecting classifying, and analyzing data.
4. Either acceptance or rejection of the hypothesis.

The scientific method involves induction of hypothesis based on observation, deduction of implications of the hypothesis, testing of the implications and confirmation or disconfirmation of the hypothesis.

In 1938 the American Philosopher John Dewey described the scientific method as a series of steps that are quite similar to steps followed in conducting educational research.

1. Clarify the main question inherent in the problem.
2. State a hypothesis—a possible answer to the question.
3. Collection, analysis and interpret information related to the question and hypothesis.
4. Form conclusions.
5. On the basis, verify or reject the hypothesis.

Despite exceptions, Dewey's explanation of scientific method remains useful in helping one to understand the research process. The scientific method is a guide or pathway what, when followed with unwavering devotion will contribute facts to any organized fund of knowledge.

Application of the Scientific Method in Education

Educational Research is the formal systematic application of the scientific method to the study of educational problems. The major difference between educational research and other scientific research is the nature of the phenomena studied. It is considerably more difficult to explain, predict and control situations involving human beings, by far the most complex of all organisms. There are so many variables, known and unknown, operating in any educational environment that it is extremely difficult to generalize or replicate findings. The kinds of rigid controls that can be established and maintained in a biochemistry lab are virtually impossible in an educational setting. Observation also difficult in an educational setting. Precise measurement is also considerably more difficult in educational research most measurement. Most be indirect, there are no instruments comparable to a barometer for measuring intelligence, achievement or attitude.

The steps involved in conducting research should look familiar since they directly parallel those of the scientific method.

(i) *Selection and Definition of a Problem:* A problem is a hypothesis or question of interest to education which can be tested or answered through the collection and analysis of data.

(ii) *Execution of Research Procedures:* The procedures reflect all the activities involved in collecting data related to the problem. For example, How data were collected and from whom? The design of the study dictates to a great extent the specific procedures involved in the study.

(iii) *Analysis of Data:* Data analysis usually involves application of one or more statistical techniques, data are analyzed in a way that permits the researcher to test the research hypothesis or answer the research question. For some studies, data analysis involves verbal synthesis of narrative data; these studies typically share resulting insights and/or generate hypothesis.

(iv) *Drawing or Stating Conclusions*: The conclusions are based on the results of data analysis. They should be stated in terms of the original hypothesis or question. Conclusions should indicate, like, whether the research hypothesis was supported or not.

For studies involving verbal synthesis, conclusions are much more tentative.

The scientific method is a set of procedures and cautions that helps one obtain reliable information for establishing facts. This is a very orderly process entitling a member of sequential steps, 1, 2, 3, 4. These steps can be applied informally in the solution of everyday problems such as the most efficient route to take from home to work or school. The more formal application of the scientific method to the solution of problems is what research is all about.

The scientific method allows an investigator to correlate his knowledge of facts and statistics with creative imagination to his attempt to make additions to the fund of organized knowledge in his discipline.

REFERENCES

1. Best, J.W. (1951). *Research in Education*, New Delhi: Prentice Hall.

2. Sprinthall, R.C. *et al.*, (1991). *"Understanding Educational Research."* USA: Prentice Hall Inc.

3. McMillan, J.H. and Sally Schumacher, S. (1989). *"Research in Education – A Conceptual Introduction"*: Second Edition. USA: Harper Collins Publishers.

4. Sukhia, S.P. (1989). *Elements of Educational Research.* Allied Publishers Pvt. Ltd.

5
Action Research

Action Research is concerned primarily with active aspect of education, when the field of research is education. In this way the work of research concerns the day to day problems that arise for the institution as whole, the student and the teacher. It aims at discovering scientific solutions for their problems.

P.M. Cook observes, "Research is a honest, exhaustive, intelligent searching for facts and their meanings or implications with reference to a given problem. The products of findings of a vivid piece of research should be an authentic, verifiable contribution to knowledge in the field studied." Hence research is search for facts, a search which has the qualities of honesty, adequacy and intelligence the results of which admit of verification and authentification. The research must be logical and objective directed at a well defined goal.

In the field of educational research is confined to problems of teaching and similar to other fields, it is scientific, objective goal oriented and verifiable. Stephen M. Corey says, "The process by which practitioners attempt to study the problems scientifically in order to guide, correct and evaluate their decisions and action is what a number of people have called Action Research."

Fundamental to Action Research

(i) Action Research is carried out scientifically.

(ii) Action Research is further carried out by workers who work in some specific field in their own capacity, so that in the educational field the research work is to be done by teachers, students, principals, etc.

(iii) Action Research is concerned with the solution of problems that come to the normal working day of a weaker. Within the single field of education, these are many aspects-curriculum, administration, communal life—The problems which require systematic research.

(iv) The object of action research is the guidance of actions and decisions, improvement and evaluation.

Importance of Action Research

The contribution that educational institutions can make to the present and future process of all democratic nations is evident, and has been realized. And if this research should be conducted into its normal functioning and descriptive solutions for its problems be found. In a normal routine day of a college, the teacher, principal and examiner have to make certain decisions and to give practical form to such decisions what these decisions should be, how such decision are to be taken, and finally how are they to do given actual shape? Action research can contribute useful information that can help in answering such questions.

Historical Background

Eventhough, there is distinct difference between basic and action research the two are intimately concerned. In this manner, action research has formed an integral part of the history of psychology, but it became a distinct entity infact only comparatively recently when educational psychology found itself a complete science. In this respect, the science of action research has a comparatively short history the extends only over a few decades. But the movement favouring it has gained in strength over the last 20-25 years.

The term denoting it was first used during the Second World War by Collier and Lewin. Their insistance upon action research was motivated by the desire to improve social relationships. Wrightstone made use of the same term in describing curricula basis. Action research was interpreted in the sense of problem solving by Taba, Robinson and Brady. Stephen M. Corey guided some very useful and important research work in the direction of action research at the Haraceman Lincoln Institute of School Experimentation, Teachers College, Columbia University, USA. During the 1920's there was a regular spate of research work in the field of education, and in this period action research attracted much attention to itself, in 1936. Buckingham published his volume, '*Research for Teachers*' and in this work he detailed the methods and objectives of research conducted by practicing teachers. From this the importance of such research work through these agencies become apparent. Action research is now an important part of a majority of educational institutions all over the world.

The following 3 elements have played a major part in its (Action Research) evolution.

1. Democratic Government.
2. Development of Scientific Consciousness.
3. Need for Improvement in Education.

Value of Action Research in India

Obviously, action research is a very important thing for a country like India. The truth of the matter is that action research is a mode of research, but even more it is a source of knowledge and learning. Action research helps to preserve democratic values and also to eliminate or reduce any mechanical or dogmatic forces working in a college. It helps the teachers, principals and examiners to evaluate their own methods and to remove their defects. On the basis of this research extra-curricular programmes can be planned in order to achieve the multiple development of students.

Very useful suggestion can be derived for the treatment of some chronic problems of schools and colleges, such as curriculum, discipline, teaching methods, extra-curricular programmes, juvenile delinquency, backwardness etc. A scientific orientation in the teachers is improved by this research so that they can organize their experiences and benefits from them. It can also help to improve the level of the students acceptance or receptivity. And finally action research also indirectly inspires everybody engaged in the work of education to work collectively for the total good.

Methodology of Action Research

1. Identification of the Problem

J.B. Best, says "Teachers will discover acres of diamonds in their own backwards, and the possessor of the inquisitive and imaginative mind may translate one of these problems is to a worth while and practicable research project." Sensitivity is essential if the problems are to be recognized and it is not found equally in all such workers. The problems of action research can be located mainly from the following sources.

(a) Problems concerning teaching.

(b) Problems concerning examination.

(c) Problems concerning extracurricular activities.

(d) Problems concerning administration and organization of institution.

Even when the above problems are existent they can be solved only when the element to be selected are necessary present. The following are the essential requirements.

1. Consciousness of the need for change and improvement.
2. Objective analysis of working conditions.
3. Critical approach to condition so that they can be properly evaluated.
4. Organization of seminars and meetings so that every aspect of the problem is highlighted.

5. Insight into the activities of the college so that the problem is clarified.

6. Knowledge of the research work done in the field of education. So that only those problems are chosen for work on which previous research is lacking.

2. *Defining and Delimiting the Problem*

It is essential that its definition should contain no word the meaning of which is not precise and clear. Hence, it is desirable that every word used to define the problem implies that its sphere should be determined because a scientific analysis of a problem is not possible if its sphere is not definite. And in defining its sphere it is essential to keep in mind the fact the problem should neither be too limited nor too widely distributed. Fig:- It is possible to conduct successful research on the absence of discipline among students forming a particular class or classes. In delimiting the problem its highest point or apex is determined. Once this apex is determined and has been fully grasped. It becomes comparatively easier to locate the basic causes that terminate in that problem.

3. *Analyzing the Causes Relevant to the Problem*

Once the problem has been designed and delimited it is analyzed in order to discover the elements, that are fundamentally responsible for the existence of the problem. For this the research worker collects much tabulated or systematic information, and when the causes are listed this information is also related to the various relevant causes. This helps to verify the causes. In analyzing the causes the following elements are taken especial note of;

(a) Logical relevance—problem should be logical relationship with case of the problem.

(b) Testable—the cause should be verifiable.

(c) Specificity—cause should specific, not general.

(d) Authenticity—cause should be rendered, authentic.

(*e*) Control—in locating the cause of the trouble another thing that should be found out is the forces that control it.

(*f*) Formulation of action hypothesis.

At these base of every research there is a definite hypothesis, and the research either establishes or disproves that hypothesis.

A good hypothesis has the following characteristics

(*i*) Verifiability.

(*ii*) Profundity of effect.

(*iii*) Clarity.

(*iv*) Purposiveness.

(*v*) Relevance to the problem.

(*vi*) Least Interference with other activities.

(*vii*) Economical.

(*viii*) Supported by pre-established theories.

(*ix*) In keeping with the abilities of the researcher.

Informing an action hypothesis assistance is forthcoming from the following sources.

(*a*) Experience

(*b*) Insight

(*c*) Creative Imagination

(*d*) Analysis of the causes of the problem

(*e*) Discussion

(*f*) Sensitivity forwards progress of the school

(*g*) Familiarity with researches

The clearer and more accurate the action hypothesis formed the greater will be changes of success. Without an accurate imagination research work of a high order is not possible.

4. *Formation of Action Hypothesis for Obtaining a Solution of the Problem*

Once the action hypothesis for the solution of a problem has been arrived at, all that immediately remains is to test it. Such a test helps to determine evidence that consists research. For this the research worker must create a definite outline of research, and in this outline all the elements effecting research are clearly stated. The main elements are,

(a) *Description of Activities:* In these outline of action hypothesis all these activities that are to be initiated are outlined in detail.

(b) *Method:* Besides the activities the outline also contains definite information concerning the direction of such activities.

(c) *Anticipated Means:* In the outline formed for the testing of his action hypothesis the research worker should clearly indicate the means or tools he will require for the successful implementation of his scheme.

(d) *Time:* In addition to the anticipated tools required, it is also necessary to make precise mention of the time required for the experiment.

5. *Evaluation of the Results of Action Research*

But the work of the research does not come to an end merely by reaching some definite conclusion. It is very true that action research is cyclical' (Stephen, M. Corey). In order to test the conclusions of one research other research projects are undertaken and this cycle progress in this manner. Unless the conclusions reached by one research project are properly tested and verified they cannot be treated as valid truths. For this the evaluation of results is essential. Without such evaluation the research worker cannot be sure that he has achieved his objective and cannot know the extent to which his research is meaningful.

The following evaluating methods are employed in order to test the validity of research test.

(a) *Observation: (i)* Fully structured, *(ii)* Semi structured, *(iii)* Free structured

(b) *Collection of Opinion:* Another method of evaluating the conclusions of action research is that of collecting opinion. In this the research can invite the opinions of teachers, students, principal and other members of his college concerning the deductions he has made in his research. But it must be clearly marked that such opinion may or may not contain any degree of objectivity. Nevertheless if a list of such deductions is published with a view to receiving opinions some benefit can accure. The least that can happen is that the researcher become aware of the opinions of other people concerning his subject of research.

(c) *Questionnaire:* More popular method of gathering the opinion of various people about the deductions from some research project is the questionnaire method. In a controlled questionnaire certain alternative answers were suggested for question asked, and the person reacting to the questionnaire is required to tick of the correct answer.

In an uncontrolled questionnaire is required to tick the voter himself. Writes down the answer of those two forms of questionnaire the controlled from is more objective, but in that case the selection of both questions and possible replies must be very judicious and perspective.

(d) *Interview:* One very simple method of verifying the deductions of a research project is to interview students, teachers, principal and other members of a college in order to ascertain their views on the subject.

(e) *Checklist:* In this a list of problems is provided and various individuals are required to check it. These people mark out the different problems that use applicable to them. A checklist to be really successful requires very considerable framing of questions.

(f) *Rating Scale:* Rating scale also used for the same purpose. In this a list of certain qualities is provided and the person-evaluating. It has to rate then according to their position. Such a scale has five or seven terms. One difficulty of this method lies in separate division of different qualities and the other in the evaluators difficulty in attaining to a conditions of complete or nearly complete objectivity rating scale method proves very useful.

(g) *Tests:* Test are various kinds such as objective tests, essay type, oral, practical tests, the teacher himself conducts these tests and the most scientific tests are objective tests.

(h) *Statistical Methods:* Sometimes statistical methods are also used to validate the conclusions drawn from some research projects.

Scope of Action Research

The scope of action research is very vast. This approach of dealing with practical problems seems to be appropriate and promising for all kinds of professional workers in education. So long as their desire in to improve their own professional practices. An administrator who is dissatisfied with his efforts to develop a higher morale in his staff could approach this problem with action research.

Advantages of Action Research

1. A person who must improve if the problem is to be solved is actively engaged in the process of improvement from the very beginning.
2. Action research emphasis a desirable decentralization of decision-making and action.

3. The research experience will broden and deepen the field workers general fund of knowledge and give him some appreciation of the powerful part research plays in fashioning our lives. It will open up on interesting new world for him.
4. As an educator, the person obliged he become sufficiently informed about research to often sound guidance to students.
5. Research will help the teacher acquire new interests, new motives and new insights that will refresh his energies and enthusiasms and revitalize his instructional procedures. Research will awaken his curiosity. Shatter some pet entrenched ideas and attitudes and make him question traditional practices. He will embark an as exciting quest for new view points and better ways of planning and guiding children's learning experiences. The thrill of working on the frontiers of knowledge, the satisfaction of experiencing continues professional growth, and the flow of personal pride and arises from doing superior work are the rich rewards that he will experience from studying research findings and applying them is the classroom.
6. There is a wide gap between research findings and their applications. Most of the studies never receive any consideration. In case the teacher himself undergoes a research experience, he will develop a better application for the research done by competent scholars and the conclusions drawn by them for their implication in the field. After having participated in action research, the teacher will play a better role in translating various research findings into practice. One's own findings are more willingly implemented.
7. Action research experience strengthens the profession as a whole. The practitioners remain helpless if they are deprived of research based theories. They cannot expect the field to gain public recognition as a full-fledged profession without building a body of

competent research. They cannot also gain the confidence of the public by practicing new educational practices without evaluating their worth. Developing a sincere interest in research will also help them establish better relationships with collegues, administrators and parents. Their enthusiasm for finding better ways of doing things will have a simulating effect on others.

8. Although most classroom teachers are applies rather than producers of research, but in future more and more of them will be called upon to play a role in research. They will have to come forward to take part in action research will enable them to read reports or summaries of research more intelligently; it will provide a foundation for more advanced study, and it may help them to prepare themselves as specialists in this field where the profession desperately needs qualified men.

9. It introduces experimental outlook among the field workers.

10. It brings decentralization in research.

Limitations of Action Research

1. It is Poor Quality Research.

   In all its aspects and steps it serves its purpose with sub-standard methods, procedures, techniques and tools. Even the participating teacher lacks in training and expertise. The level of work and outcome gets diluted in the hands of an ill-equipped and unprepared research worker. George A. Mouly says "Action research can became a case of the blind leading the blind and the problem is further aggravated by the fact that teachers generally are too close to their problems and too intrained in scientific objectivity to be vigourous and objective in their approach."

2. It is an unduly localized research effort.

The generalizations cannot acquire a universal validity. The applicability of findings to another class and another school is quiet doubtful.

3. It may become an additional burdon on an already overburdened teacher.

4. Because of numerous limitations, it may produce wrong and unverifiable conclusions.

Once the work of evaluation is satisfactory concluded, general laws can be derived from the conclusions drawn from the result of action research and these general laws can be employed to improve educational institutions. They also help to formulate further action research. The actual method of research is quite apparent from the foregoing account of different steps in the action research method. All these various steps are intimately related.

REFERENCES

1. Corey, S.M. (1953). *Action Research to Improve School Practices.* New York: Teachers College, Columbia University.

2. Mc Burney, Donald, H. (2001). *Research Methods.* Australia: Wordsworth.

6

Case Study

Introduction

The central question of educational research is, "how can knowledge of the ways in which children learn and the means by which schools achieve this goals be verified, built upon and extended?" There are two broad approaches to educational researches for the verification and cumulation of educational knowledge. The first is based on scientific paradigm, rests upon the creation of theoretical framework that can be tested by experimentation, replication and refinement. The second alternate perspective is interpretative and subjective approach which can be best explored by case study method.

Case Study—Meaning and Significance

Case study mean an intensive analysis of many important aspects of an individual, a situation or an institution. The foremost purpose of case study is to gain a clear perspective of the past and the present. The present problems are understandable only on the basis of the past. It helps to develop an understanding of the deep routed causes of the present problem. A case study is more than an expanded cumulative record. It contains interpretations, recommendations and reports in follow up work.

The case study is concerned with everything that is significant in the history or development of the case. The case may be of an individual person, a family, a group, a social institution or a social community. In a case study, a deep probe is made into the interaction between the factors that produce change on the subject matter under study. The case study method aims at studying everything about something. According to P.V. Young, case study is method of exploring and analyzing the life of a social unit, be that a person, a family, an institution, cultural group or even an entire community.

Case study method is different from survey method. The survey method is generally based on large cross-sectional samples while case studies are oriented to the more intensive and longitudinal study of a smaller sample.

Definition of Case Study

"Case study is the way of organizing social data so as to preserve the unitary character of the social object being studied. Expressed somewhat differently, it is an approach which views any social unit as a whole."

– Goode and Hatt

"Case study method may be defined as a small inclusive and intensive study of an individual in which investigator brings to bear all his skill and method or as systematic gathering of enough information about a person to permit one to understand how he or she functions as a unit of the society."

– Yang Hsin Pao

The case study is a form of qualitative analysis involving the very careful and complete observation of a person, situation or an institution.

– Biesanz

Characteristics of Case Study Method

Unlike the experimenter who manipulates variables to determine their casual significance or the surveyor who asks standardized questions of large, representative samples, the case study researcher typically observes the characteristics of an individual unit—a child, a clique, a class, a school or the community. The purpose of such observation is to probe deeply and to analyze intensively the multifarious phenomena that constitute the life cycle of the unit with a view to establishing generalizations about the wider population to which that unit belongs. The important characteristics of case study method are:

1. It should be based on adequate and complete data.
2. Data of the case study should be valid.
3. Data should have continuity in it.
4. Data should be scientifically synthesized.
5. Data should be kept confidential.
6. Follow up work must be taken up.
7. The unit of study is an individual, family, institution or an entire community.
8. The aim of case study is deep and detailed study of the unit.
9. It is mainly qualitative in character.

Steps of Case Study Method

The case study method includes the following steps:

1. Selection of the case or cases.
2. Determining initial status or symptoms.
3. Formation of hypothesis.
4. Collection of explanatory data.
5. Diagnosis and identification of casual factors.
6. Remedial or developmental treatment.
7. Follow up or re-checking.

Uses of Case Study

The use of the case study method are:

1. The case study method is a useful mode of investigation into the casual relationships of complex educational phenomenon.
2. It is frequently employed in studying cases of problem children, maladjusted students and students showing academic and other difficulties.
3. It is also employed in finding out the general characteristics of phenomenon of a given class or an area.
4. Case study method is employed in studying the teaching difficulties of beginning teachers.
5. Case study method has been extended in the investigation or normal and gifted children.
6. Case study method can be employed to find out the factors which are responsible for successful institution and groups.
7. Case study has been extended to the investigation of ideal teachers.
8. Case study method forms the basis of guidance in preventing maladjustment.
9. It is an important source of educational programmes and reforms.
10. Case study helps in formulating valid generalization.
11. Case study enlarges the range of personal experience of the research.
12. It is possible to locate deviant cases.

Limitations of Case Study

Through the case study method have the above mentioned advantages, the case study method have the following limitations also. They are:

1. The first and foremost difficulty is the overconfidence that the researcher develops in this mind. The researcher so begins to feel as if he knows everything about the individual and needs no further enlightenment.
2. Generalization are drawn from too few cases is not applicable to all cases in a population.
3. It is very difficult to select subjects on units for a study that are representative or typical.
4. Sources of data may not be reliable.
5. Sources of data may be reliable but data may suffer from over emphasis on unusual events or distortion.
6. Subjective bias is a threat to objective data gathering and analysis.
7. Effects may be wrongly attributed to factors that are merely associated rather than cause and effect related.
8. For using this method effectively, the researcher must be thoroughly familiar with the existing knowledge of the field of enquiry and should be skillful in isolating the significant variables from the irrelevant variables.
9. There is enough scope for errors due to inaccurate observation and faulty inference, selection of a case that is not typical of the group, errors in reporting, failure of memory, repression of unpleasant facts etc. Under such conditions the data collection and the inferences drawn are at times for from being valid.
10. The research may develop a tendency towards adhoc-theory is in place of finding some significant explanations to a particular phenomena, he tries to find some commonsense explanations to it.
11. The time and money needed for case study is much greater than in other methods.

12. Subject may write what he thinks and what the investigator wants. The greater the rapport, the more subjective the whole process is.

13. The subject is more likely to be self justificatory than factful.

14. The literacy touch results in romantic over and under statement, convenient forgetting etc.

Conclusion

While conducting a case study, every possible care should be taken to ensure the validity of the research. For that possible steps should be taken to avoid common sources of in accuracies as errors in perception, falsification of memory, unconscious omissions, tendency to dramatic, projection of one's own ideas, attitudes, values and the like. Inclination to pay special attention to unusual and striking incidents and to neglect common place and small details.

REFERENCES

1. Varma, M. (1965). *An Introduction to Education and Psychological Research.* Bombay: Asia Publishing House.
2. Mouly, G.J. (1964). *The Science of Educational Research.* New Delhi: McGraw Hill.
3. Vandalen, D.D. (1968). *Understanding Educational Research.* New York: McGraw Hill.
4. Whitney, B. (1950). *Elements of Research.* Bombay: Asia Publishing House.
5. Rummell, F.J. (1964). *An Introduction to Research Procedures in Education.* New York: Harper and Row Publishers.
6. Fox, David, J. *The Research Process in Education.*

7
Correlational Research

Introduction

When the relationship is of a quantitative nature, the appropriate statistical tool for discovering and measuring the relationship and expressing it in a brief formula is known as *correlation*. It is a analysis of the co-variation between two or more variables. Variable is a concept a noun that stands for variation with in a class of objects. If all members of a class are identical, we do not have a variable. Such characteristics are called *constants*.

Types of Correlation

(a) *Positive and Negative Correlation:* A positive correlation means high scores on the one variable tend to be associated with high scores on other variable. A negative correlation means high scores on the one variable is associated with low scores on the other variable and low scores on the one are associated with high scores on the either.

(b) *Linear and Non Linear:* The correlation between two variable is said to be linear if corresponding to a unit change in one variable, there is a constant change in other variable over entire range of values. The relationship between two variables is said to be non-linear if corresponding to a unit change in first variable, the other variable does not change at a constant rate, but at fluctuating rate.

Correlational Research

Correlational research is the casual comparative research. In it the relationship among two or more variables are studied without any attempt to influence them. A correlational study describes the degree to which two or more quantitative variables are related it does so by the use of 'r'. The basic design of correlational research is simple and involves collecting two or more scores of the same group of subjects and computing 'r'. Those involving complex relationship utilize multiple and partial correlations in order to provide a dearer picture of the relationship being investigated.

Purpose of Correlational Research

1. To clarify our understanding of important phenomena through the identification of relationship among variables.

2. If a relationship of sufficient magnitude exists between 2 variables it becomes possible to predict a score on the either variable, if the score on the other variable is known. The variable that is used to make prediction is called *predictor variable,* the variable about which prediction is made is called *criterion variable.*

Basic Steps in Correlational Research

Problem Selection

The variables to be included in a correlational study should be chosen based on a sound rationable growing out of experience of theory. The researcher should have some reason for thinking certain variables may be related. The clarity in defining variables will avoid many problems later on. The major types of problems are the focus of correlational studies.

1. Is the variable X related to variable Y

2. How well does variable P Predict variable C

3. What are the relationships among a larger number of variable and what predictions can be made that are based on them.

Sample

The sample for a correlational study as in any type of study should be selected carefully and if possible randomly. The first step in selecting a sample of course is to identify an appropriate population one that is meaningful and from which data on each of the variables of interest can be collected. The minimum acceptable sample size for a correlational study is considered by most researchers to be not less than 30. Samples larger than 30 are much more likely to provide meaningful results.

Instruments

The instruments used are Rating Scale, Interview tally sheets, flowcharts, performance checklists, Anecdotal records etc. They give quantitative data. As with any study whatever instruments are used must yield reliable scores.

Design and Procedures-- Subjects: A B C D E ....
Observations: O_1, O_2, O_3 ......

Two or more scores are obtained from each individual in the sample, one score for each variable of interest. Pairs of scores are then correlated and the resulting correlation co-efficient indicates the degree of relationship between the variables.

Data Collection

In a relationship study, all the data on both variables will usually be collected within a fairly short time. For example, If the researcher is interested in increasing the relationship between verbal aptitude and memory, a test of verbal aptitude and another of memory would be administered closely together in time to the same group of subjects.

Data Analysis and Interpretation

'r' will be a decimal it lies between –1 and +1. The closer co-efficient is to +1 or –ve 1, the stronger the relationship. If the sign is +ve, the relationship is +ve and vice versa. Correlations within the range (0.20 to 0.35) show only very slight relationship between variables although they may be statistically significant. A correlation of 0.20 shows that only 4 per cent of the variance is common to the two measures. Correlations within the range (0.35 to 0.65) are statistically significant beyond 1 per cent level.

When correlations are around 0.40 crude group production may be possible. Correlation within the range (0.65 to 0.85) make possible group predictions that are accurate enough for most purposes. Nearer the top of the range, group predictions can be made accurately usually predicting the proportion of successful candidates in selection problems within a very small margin of error. Near the top of this correlation range individual predictions can be made that are considerably more accurate than would occur if no such selection procedures were used. Correlations over. A correlation of 0.85 indicates that the measure used for prediction has about 72 per cent variance in common with the performance being predicted. When correlations at this level are obtained however they are very useful for either individual or group prediction.

Conclusion

Correlational studies provide an estimate of just how related 2 variables are. If two variables are highly related a 'r' nearer to + 1 will be obtained of 2 variables are not related a 'r' near 0.00 will be obtained. The more highly related two variables are the more accurate are predictions based on their relationship while relationships are rarely perfect a number of variables are sufficiently related to permit useful prediction.

REFERENCES

1. L.R. Gay, *Educational Research.*
2. James H. McMillan, *Research in Education.*
3. Louis Cohen and Lawrence Manion, *Research Methods in Education.*

8

Selection of Research Problem: Detection of Research Areas

The Research Problem

Society is encountered by several problems which needed to be studied for finding a solution. The aim of research is to improve the standard of living in the society. A research problem is exactly that a problem that someone could like to research. A problem can be anything that a person find unsatisfactory or unsetting a difficulty of some sort, a sort of affairs that need to be unchanged or changed. A research problem refers to some kind of problem which a researcher experiences or observes in the context of either a theoretical or practical situation and wants to obtain a solution for the same.

The first step in the research process is the choice of a suitable problem for investigation. The identification of a research problem is a difficult but an important phase of the entire research process. It requires a great deal of patience and logical thinking on the part of the researcher. A problem must spring from the researchers mind like a plant springing from its own seed.

Knowing the Field

It is first necessary for a researcher to choose a broad field within which he will conduct the study. The researcher should have a deep interest in the field. His enthusiasm and real curiosity enhance his motivation for the successful completion of the study. The field selected should be one in which the researcher is capable of demonstrating necessary initiative, originality and good adjustment. A thorough understanding of the known facts and ideas in the field or area in which the researcher is interested constitutes the first and most important step in selecting a problem for study. If the researcher, is familiar with his field and known what studies have already been conducted in it, he will also known about the problems which have remained unsolved.

A survey of suggestions for further research given at the end of research reports and reviews of research is helpful to the researcher in getting an idea about the gaps which exists in knowledge in a particular field of educational research. Periodicals and bibliographies which appear in most field of educational research are helpful in keeping the researcher informed about the research going on in the field in which he has competence and interest.

Selection of the Problem

One problem may be selected rather than the

(*i*) because of its interest

(*ii*) as a basis for further study

(*iii*) to improve educational conditions

(*iv*) to further personal ambitions

A research worker should be aware of the whole picture of the educational research-completed, under progress, and needed. In order to discover the problem he has to get acquainted with the field through an approach to varied sources in the form of books, courses, periodicals, proceedings of learned societies, list of thesis historical analyses, reports of conferences, survey of scientific studies of all kinds and so on.

The following points may be observed by a researcher in selecting a research problem or a subject for research.

(i) Subject which is overdone should not be normally chosen, for it will be a difficult task to throw any new light in such a case.

(ii) Controversial subject should not become the choice of an average researcher.

(iii) Too narrow or too questions should be avoided.

(iv) The subject selected for research should be familiar and feasible so that the related research material or sources of research are within one's reach.

(v) The importance of the subject, the qualifications and training of a researcher, the costs involved, the time factors are few other criteria that must also be considered in selecting a problem.

(vi) The selection of a problem must be preceded by a preliminary study. This may not be necessary the problem requires the conduct of a research closely similar to one that has already been done.

Before the final selection of the problem, a researcher must ask himself,

1. Whether he is well equipped in terms of his background to carryout the research?
2. Whether the study falls within the budget he can afford?
3. Whether the necessary co-operation can be obtained from those who must participate in research?

If the subject for research is selected properly by observing the above mentioned points, the research will not be boring drudgery, rather it will be love's labour. The subject or the problem selected must involve the researcher and must have an uppermost place in his mind so that he may undertake all pains needed for the study.

The first step in selecting a problem is to identify a general problem area that is related to our area of expertise and of particular interest to us. The next step is to narrow down the general problem area to a specific researchable problem. A well defined manageable problem results in a well defined manageable study.

Detection of Research Areas

The major sources of a research problem are as follows:

1. Professional Experience

One of the most fruitful sources of problems for the researcher is his own experience as professional educator. In the classroom there is a dynamic interaction between teacher and pupil, between pupil and pupil, and between pupil, and materials. This interaction provides a rich source of problems to be solved through education research. Classroom lectures an discussions suggest many stimulating problems to be solved.

The teacher may be confronted with a number of behavioural problems in the classroom. He has to make decisions about the probable effects of classroom instruction on pupil behaviour so as to establish a relationship between instructional objectives, learning experiences and pupil change. The pupil behaviour may be analyzed in terms of his achievement, interest, attitudes, intelligence, aptitudes, motivation and personality.

The teacher has to make decisions about teaching methods and techniques. He may study the effectiveness of a particular method of teaching so as to base classroom instructions upon empirical evidence rather than upon its biased impressions.

The classroom is not the only source of problems for the teacher. The experience of the pupils, their aptitudes, home environment, peer influences, socio economic status and motivational level are rich sources of problems. The educational administrators may find subjects of research in the areas concerning decision making, scheduling, teacher placements, instructional supervision, and several other matters with which they are concerned.

Contacts and discussions with research oriented people, attending conferences, seminars and listening to the learned speakers are helpful in identifying research areas. Active membership in organizations, which are concerned with the improvement of educational system usually, brings one into close contact with crucial problems and issues concerning education.

2. *Inference from Theory*

A second important source of research problem lies in the inferences that can be drawn from various educational and psychological theories known to the researcher. The application of general principles involved in various theories to specific classroom situations makes an excellent starting point for research. Learning theories, personality theories, theories of intelligence, theories of motivation, sociological theories and many others provide rich sources of topics for research in classroom situations.

While there are several major sources of problems, the most meaningful ones are generally those derived from theory. Problems derived form a theoretical problem area are not only preferable in terms of contribution to true scientific progress in education, they also facilitate the formulation of hypothesis based on a sound rationale; these hypothesis in turn facilitate ultimate interpretation of study results. The result of a study based on a theoretical problem contribute to their related theory by confirming or disconfirming some aspect of the theory and also by suggesting additional studies that needed to be done.

3. *Professional Literature*

Among the sources of problems, one has to be thoroughly acquainted with the literature in the field of one's interest. The study of professional literature will not only expose a researcher to pressing research problems, but also suggest the way in which research is conducted. Research reports, bibliographies of books and articles, periodicals, research abstracts, year books, dictionaries and research guides suggest areas that needed research. Some specialized sources as the 'Encyclopaedia of Educational Research', 'Dissertation Abstracts International', 'The Handbook of Research on Teaching' and similar publications provide rich sources of problems.

The publications like "Educational Research", "Surveys of Research in Education" are exclusively devoted to identifying and bringing into sharp focus the varied research needs in the different areas and aspects of Indian education. All published research reports generally conclude by making suggestions about further research.

Replication or extension of completed research studies is also a profitable and worthwhile activity for a beginner research. Repeating a study at different times on different groups and in different places increases the extent to which the research findings can be generalized and provides additional evidence of the validity of the findings.

4. *Technological and Social Changes*

Technological and social changes demand development of new courses and curriculum for students, in educational institutions. All these developments constantly bring forth new problems for research. The use of hardware and software in classroom instruction, the training of teachers in the methodology of teaching through team teaching, micro teaching, etc. are being advocated by the educationists all over the country. The development of commercial and educational television is a new factor in the field of education. How will it alter the role of the classroom teacher has to be decided on the basis of careful research. The unemployment of the educated and allround corruption are some social factors which are upsetting the steady programmes of education. The research worker should therefore search for the solution of these problems.

5. *Discussions*

Classroom discussions, seminars and exchange of ideas with the faculty members and fellow scholars and students will suggest many stimulating problems to be solved. Close professional relationship, academic discussions and constructive academic climate are especially advantageous opportunities.

6. Questioning Attitude

A questioning attitude towards prevailing practices and research oriented academic experience will effectively promote problem awareness.

7. Consultations

Consultation with an expert, research supervisors, research guide, a course instructor or a senior scholar will be helpful.

8. Casual observations are rich sources of problems.

9. Current Political Issues are rich sources of problems.

10. Personal Experience and Insights may suggest research problems that should be examined more in depth.

Questions One Need to Ask When Selecting a Problem

The following questions should asked before selecting a problem.

1. Is the problem researchable?
2. *Is it interesting:* For if it seems dull and boring to the research worker, there is little hope that he would do justice.
3. *Is it new?:* For if it has been already tackled by some previous researcher, then the duplication of the effort would be waste.
4. *Is it significant?:* For if it is not worthwhile, if it neither adds to knowledge nor leads to any improvement in the current practices, it would be waste.

5. *Is it feasible?*: For a problem may be interesting, significant and new and yet not be a good problem for a particular research workers, then he may fail to carry it to a successful conclusion. One must ask therefore,

   (*a*) Do I possess the necessary competence to plan and carry out a study of the type this problem warrants? Have I got enough knowledge about the field and sufficient skill to manipulate the required tools and techniques for gathering and interpreting data?

   (*b*) Are valid and reliable data gathering devices and procedures available?

   (*c*) Will I be able to get proper guidance from a staff or a faculty member in planning and completing the task?

   (*d*) Do I have necessary financial resources to carry out the study?

   (*e*) Do I have enough time to executive the project from beginning to end?

   (*f*) Do I have courage and determination to pursue the study inspite of some difficulties and social hazards that may be involved in it?

It is only when the above questions are answered in the affirmative, that the problem can be considered as a good one.

To find out his interest in the problem, the following questions may be asked.

(*a*) Do I have merely a passive curiosity in the solution of problem?

(*b*) Is my interest present because of any anticipated rewards?

(*c*) Is my interest so strong that it might involve strong bias in seeking the solution of the problem?

One might consider the following questions in determining the value of a topic.

(a) Is it likely the results of the study will add to the present body of knowledge or will it only duplicate?

(b) Does the field need re-working?

(c) Are the results that may be obtained of practical value?

(d) Who might be interested in the results?

Characteristics of a Good Research Problem

The basic characteristic of a research problem is that it is 'researchable'. A researchable problem is one that can be investigated through the collection and analysis of the data. Problems relating to philosophical or ethical issues are not researchable. Another major characteristic of a good problem is that it has theoretical or practical significance. A third major characteristic of a good problem is that it is a good problem for the researcher. It must be a problem that the researcher can adequately investigate.

Conclusion

A research problem is one which requires a researcher to find out the best solution for the given problem, into find out by which course of action the object can be attained optimally in the context of a given environment. In order to discover the problems, one has to get acquainted with the field through an approach to varied sources in the form of books, courses, periodicals, list of thesis, historical analyses, reports of conference etc.

REFERENCES

1. Kothari, C.R. *Research Methodology, Methods and Techniques.* Wishwa Prakasan Publishers.
2. Sukhia, S.P. (1989). *Elements of Educational Research.* Allied Publishers Pvt. Ltd.
3. Gay, L.R. (1996). *Educational Research – Competencies for Analysis and Application.* New York.

4. McMillan, J.H. and Schumacker, S. (1989). *Research in Education – A Conceptual Introduction.* Harper Collins Publishers.

5. Cohen, L. and Manion, L. (1994). *Research Methods in Education.*

6. Koul, L. (1997). *Methodology of Educational Research.*

7. Sidhu, K.S. (1992) *Methodology of Research in Education.* Sterling Publishers Pvt. Ltd.

8. Wallen, N. and Frankel, J.P. *How to Design and Evaluate Research in Education.* New York.

9
Sources of Information

Internet, Search Engines, Websites, E-mail etc.

A researcher needs to acquire up-to-date information related to his research problem. Internet, search engines, websites, e-mails etc. help very much in the information gathering process by saving time and effort of the researcher.

Internet

The Internet is simply a collection of computers around the world that communicate with each other over telephone lines. People can use the information on the network and also add information to it.

The Internet is Not a Library

Since anybody can put information on the net the research have to evaluate the information from the Internet. In order to ensure the authorship the researcher has to ask the following questions.

1. Is the author a well-known authority?
2. If not, is the author's work cited approvingly by a known authority?
3. If not, can you find biographical information that could validate the authors credentials?

Websites

'A computer screen of information is called a web page. The combined web pages constitute a website. Every web page has a unique address called URL (Uniform Resource Locator). These are often very long and contain numbers, letters, punctuations etc. For eg:- The URL address of the American Psychological Association's website is www.apa.org

Proprietary Websites

A proprietary website is one has as privately owned and accessible only by permission, usually for a fee. Your user name and password helps to access these proprietary sources.

Eg:

1. The Web of Science
2. Info Trac
3. Psych Info and Psych LIT Psychological Sources

Search Engines

A search engine is a specialized device that searches the World Wide Web for documents that match key words, proper names and phrases.

Eg: Yahoo, Alta Vista, Hotbot, Infoseek, Lycos, Web-crawler, goto, excite, google, etc.

Each search engine has its own weaknesses and strength. This problem can be overcome by using a meta engine like Meta Crawler that searches the output of several other search engines. URL address is www.metacrawler.com.

E-mail

It is the most commonly used interest service. E-mail is rapidly replacing the postal service as a preferred means of written communication at a distance.

Advantages of E-mail

1. It is almost instantaneous when compared to other messaging mediums like fax.

2. It directly reaches the concerned individual's E-mail box.
3. It ensures a much higher degree of security or privacy because only an authorized person can open and even known the presence of the mail.
4. Compared to other systems it is dirtcheap that is, it is a economical service.
5. It does not want the recipient "on the spot."

People seem to respond to E-mail much more promptly than to either a phone message or a letter. So E-mail has encouraged communication between researchers. Most authors include their E-mail address in all publications.

REFERENCES

1. Sivarajan, K. *et. al.*, (2006). *Information and Communication Technology and Communicative English*. Calicut University: Central Co-op Stores Ltd.
2. Das, S.K. (2005). *A Text Book of Information Technology*, New Delhi: Dominant Publishers and Distributors.

10

Selecting and Evaluating Problems; Statement of the Problem

Society is encountered by several problems which need to be studied for finding a solution. The aim of research is to improve the standard of living in the society. Their need the attention of the researcher.

A research problem is exactly that a problem that someone would like to research. A problem can be anything that a person finds unsatisfactory or unsettling, a difficulty of some sort, a state of affairs that need to be changed, anything this is not working as well as it might. A research problem refers to some kind of problem which a researcher experiences or observes in the context of either a theoretical or practical situation and wants to obtain a solution for the sake.

Selection of the Problem

To begin with, the researcher has to decide the general idea or the aspect of the subject matter he would like to enquire into it may be based on some practical considerations or by some theoretical and intellectual interest. A research topic may be selected from the burning problems of the time. A problems must spring from the researcher's mind like a plant springing from its own seed. The researcher may select problems rather than other,

- Because of its interest
- As a basis of further study

- To improve educational conditions
- To further personal ambitions
- To fill the gaps in the field

In order to select problem, he has to get acquainted with the field through varied sources in the farm of books, courses, periodicals, list of thesis, historical analyses, survey of scientific studies of all kinds, reports of conferences and so on.

Problems involve areas of concern to researchers as educators, conditions they want to improve, difficulties they want to eliminate, questions for which they seek answers. Usually, a research problem is initially posed as a question, which serves as the focus of researchers investigation.

To sum up, the selection of research problem has high value to the society and the researcher must be able to identify those problem that need urgent solutions.

Criteria for Selecting and Evaluating Research Problem

'Problems are solutions in disagree'. The most important aspect a researcher should keep in mind while selecting a problem is to clearly define the problem. It is said that 'a problem clearly stated is a problem half solved'.

While selecting and evaluating a research problem the criteria to be considered are.

1. Clear and Unambiguous

There must be perfect clarify in the problem taken for study. It should not give scope for divergent expressions and thus become confusing. The focus of any research investigation is the problem. i.e., what exactly is being investigated? Researchers have to be specific about the terms and phrases used in the research study.

Since research questions is the focus of a research problem or investigation, it is particularly important that the question is clear.

For example, 'is a humanistically oriented classroom *effective*?' The terms in the research question should be clearly defined, i.e., whether effective means 'results in increased academic proficiency' or 'results in happier children' or 'costs less money' or 'makes life easier for teachers'.

There are 3 ways to clarify the terms in research questions.

1. To use a constitutive definition-referred to as dictionary approach.
2. To clarify by example.
3. To define the terms operationally-activities or operations necessary to measure or identify the term must be specified.

The researchers will not know what to look for if they are under about the meaning of key terms in research questions. So the problem should be clear and unambiguous.

2. *Logical and Systematic*

Research is guided by logic or reasoning. The researcher must be able to establish relationships in a logical manner. Similarly, the problem must be amenable for study in a specified sequence in accordance with well defined set of rules and methods. Systematic method rejects the use of guess and intuitions in arriving at conclusions. In research, the commonly accepted method for arriving generalizations are of two types viz.,

- Logical method
- Statistical method

Inductive method

Deductive method

The logical method are useful in the study of cause and effect relationships. Statistical methods are based on sampling or sample survey method.

3. *Feasibility*

A research problem is one that can be investigated with available resources. Questions involving space exploration (For example: the study of long-term effects of special programmes like Head—Start) requires great deal of time and money. Most of the researches in educational institutions is likely to be done by 'outsiders' often university professors and students only if funded by temporary grants. Lack of feasibility limits research efforts.

After the research problem has been evaluated, there remains the problem of suitability for a particular researcher. Some questions to be considered by researcher are:

- Am I competent to plan and carry out the study? Do I know enough about this field, to understand its significant aspects and to interpret my findings. Am I skilful enough to develop administer and interpret the necessary data gathering devices and procedures?
- Are pertinent data accessible? Are valid and reliable data gathering during and procedures available? Will school authorities permit me to contact the students, conduct experiments, administer necessary tests, interview teachers or have to access to important cumulative records?
- Will I have financial resources to carry out the study? If the project is an expensive one what is the possibility of getting a grant from philanthropic foundation or from governmental agencies such as University Grants Commission?
- Will I have enough time to complete the project? Will there be time to device the procedures, select data gathering devices, gather and analyze the data and complete research report?
- Will I have the courage and determination to pursue the study inspite of the difficulties and social hazards that may be involved? Will I be willing to work aggressively when the data are difficult together and others are reluctant to co-operate? If these are answered

affirmative the research problem can be considered as good one?

For a problem may be interesting, significant and new and yet not be a good problem for a research worker and he may fail to carry it through to a successful conclusion. So the researcher should consider the feasibility, while selecting and evaluating a problem.

4. Empirical

Research is always related with one or more aspects of real situation and hence deals with concrete data that provides a basis for external validity to research results. Hence, the problem should be such as to take realities into consideration. It is only through this process that knowledge gets accumulated and society is benefited.

5. Relation Between Variables

The research problem selected for study should express a relation between the variables. The problem under study must be in a position to highlight the nature, extend and implication of such relation existing among variables of the study. A suggested relationship means that two qualities or characteristics are tied together or connected in some way. For example, 'Are motivation and learning related? If so how?'

6. Verifiable

Verifiability is said to be the major criterion of researches in physical and natural sciences. Though results of research studies in social sciences cannot be reproduced, research work should be undertaken with the intention to make the study useful and replicable.

7. Significant and Interesting

The problem selected must be interesting and significant, that is, it is worth investigating because it will contribute important knowledge unless the problem is interesting, the researcher may lose interest in the middle. The co-operation of the respondents also varies depending on how it is interesting to them.

8. Ethical

The question in the research problem must be ethical. It shall not cause physical or psychological harm or damage to human beings, or to natural or social environment of which they are a part.

The following points may be observed by the researcher while selecting and evaluating a research problem.

- Subject which is overdone should not be normally chosen, for it will be a difficult task.
- Controversial subject should not become a choice of an average researcher.
- Too narrow or too vague problems should be avoided.
- The subject selected from research must be familiar and feasible, so that the selected materials are within one's reach.
- The importance of the subject, qualification and training of a researcher, time factors are the few other criteria that must also be considered in selecting a problem.
- The selection of a problem must be preceded by a preliminary survey or pilot study.

The criteria for selection of a problem and standards for its evaluation may be summarized into four principles in terms of personal interest, personal capabilities, values of topic and availability of data.

To find out researchers interest in the problem, the following questions may be asked:

1. Do I have merely passive curiosity in the solution of my problem?
2. Is my interest so strong that it might involve strong bias in seeking the solution of the problem?

To determine the value of a topic following questions should be considered:

1. Is it likely that results of study will add present body of knowledge?
2. Does the field need reworking?
3. Are there gaps in verified knowledge that need to be filled?
4. Who might be interested in the results?

To find out whether the topic is within the researchers capabilities, he might ask:

1. Am I equipped with specialized skills, knowledge and capabilities for solving the problem?
2. Is the topic such that it will be possible for me to get adequate sponsorship?

Finally researcher should investigate the availability of data to obtain satisfactory answers for the following question:

1. Are the particular data, necessary in the solution of the topic, accessible to me?
2. Are the techniques necessary for the solution of the topic developed to the extend that the conclusions will not have to be so qualified as to make them of little or no value?
3. Can the topic be limited sufficiently due to lack of availability of data to permit satisfactory treatment?

It is only when the above questions are answered in the affirmative, the problem can be considered as a good one for research investigation.

To sum up a research problem rightly and rationally selected helps researcher to complete the project within the prescribed time limit and budgeted amount. The right selection of research problem will boost the moral of the researcher, provides intellectual satisfaction, and benefits society.

Statement of the Problem

Statement of a problem indicates the variables of interest to researcher and the specific relationship between those variables which is to be investigated. It is usually a declarative statement but in the question form.

According to Whiteny, after the problem has been selected, the next task is to define it in a form amenable to research. "To define a problem means to put a fence around it, to separate it by careful distinctions from like questions found in related situations of need." The researcher must be certain that he knows exactly what his problem is before he begins to work on it. Specifying a problem explicitly and narrowing it down to workable size are extremely important at the very start.

According to Munroe and Engelhart, to define a problem means to specify it in detail and with precision. Each question and subordinate question to be answered is to be specified. The limits of investigation must be determined. It is necessary to review previous studies and related literatures in order to determine just what is to be done.

The researcher is required to describe the background of the study, its theoretical basis and underlying assumptions and state the problem in concrete, specific and workable questions. A good statement of problem must clarify what is to be determined or solved. It must restrict the scope to specific and workable questions and the variables in the research questions should be defined in operational terms. Personal observation and experience may be basis of a problem. A cause and effect relationship may be suggested on the basis of theory and previous research findings. Some examples of problem statements are:

- Racial segregation have damaging effect upon self image of minority group of children.
- Participation in high school competitive athletics may be detrimental to academic achievement.

These problem statements involve more than information gathering. They suggest answers or conclusions and provide basis of research activity. There are two ways of stating a problem;

1. Posing question or questions.
2. Making declarative statement or statements.

The question form has an advantage in sharpening and focusing the issue, but the declarative form is common, and both ways may be combined easily in an initial statement.

A well written problem statement, defines all relevant variables either directly or operationally. Operational definition define concepts in terms of operations or processes and it is a helpful way to clarify the meaning. The operational definition of variables helps to narrow the scope of general question to specific measurable and observable variables.

The problem should be stated in such a way that it indicates a relation between two or more variables. It should neither involve philosophical issues nor values or judgemental questions that cannot be answered by a scientific investigator.

Conclusion

To conclude, in every research activity, the first and foremost step happens to be that of selecting and properly defining a research problem, so that it becomes susceptible to research. The researcher should finalize the problem only after considering all possible criteria's of good research viz., novelty, significance, feasibility, availability of data, guidance and other facilities, creativity, coverage etc. At first the problem is stated in a general way, the ambiguities are resolved, thinking and rethinking process results in specific formulation of problem so that it becomes realistic and meaningful, thereby paving the way for benefit of humanity.

REFERENCES

1. Kerlinger, D. *Research in Behavioural Science.*
2. Koul, L. (2002). *Methodology of Educational Research,* New Delhi: Vikas Publishing Co.
3. Gay, L.R. (1996). *Educational Research,* New York: Prentice Hall.
4. Chandra, S.S. and Sharma, K. (1997). *Research in Education.* New Delhi: Atlantic Publications.

11
Variables

Introduction

A variable is some aspect of a testing condition that can change or take on different characteristics with different conditions. In other words, a variable is a concept—a noun that stands for variation within a class of objects, such as chair, gender, eye, colour, achievement, motivation or running speed. Even "Spunk", "Style" and "Lust for life" are variables. Notice that the individual member in the class of objects, however, must differ—or vary—to qualify the class are identical, we do not have a variable. Such characteristics are called *constants,* since the individual members of the class are not allowed to vary, but rather are held constant. In any study some characteristics will be variables, while others will be constants.

The variables are tangible: duration, frequency, or intensity of bar presses; items checked on a questionnaire; murders committed; book written. The theoretical concepts of means of the operational definitions used to measure the concepts. To test this theory, you must take the theoretical concepts of anxiety and affiliation motive and relate them to variables in the real world by meant of operational definitions. The theory is an abstract statement. You can measure anxiety by the Taylor Manifest Anxiety scale and affiliation by how close people sit to each other in the experiment. These two measures constitute the variables of the study. It is the scores on the variable of anxiety and distance apart that are related to one another as tests of the hypothesis. The relationship between the variables is taken as providing support for or against the particular theory that generated the experiment. Variable are the conditions or characteristics that the experimenter manipulates, controls, or observes.

Types of Variables

There are many type of variables are used and discussed in psychological research. They are:

(i) Dependent and Independent Variables

(ii) Confounded Variables

(iii) Qualitative and Categorical Variables

(iv) Continuous and Discrete Variables

(v) Manipulated and Outcome Variables

Dependent and Independent Variables

The most basic distinction among variables is between dependent variables and independent variables. The dependent variables is a measure of the behaviour of the subject that reflects the effects of the independent variable. In the language of stimulus-response psychology, it is the response. We call it the dependent variable because it depends (we hope) on the value of another variable (the independent variable).

The independent variable is the condition manipulated or selected by the experimenter to determine its effect on behaviour. It is the stimulus of stimulus-response psychology. According to the famous frustration-aggression law, frustration causes aggression. We could test the frustration-aggression law by promising students a reward for completing a certain task. The students would be divided into two groups. We could give one group the reward but give the other group some excuse why they wouldn't get the promised reward. If the frustrated group rated the task less fun than the non-frustrated group, then we would confirm the hypothesis. Here the independent variable is whether students were given the promised reward. The dependent variable is their rating of how much fun the task was.

Every independent variable has at least two values. The different values of an independent variable is called levels. In educational research an independent variable may be a particular teaching method, a type of teaching material, a reward, or a period of exposure to a particular condition, or an attribute such as sex or level of intelligence. The dependent variable may be a test score, the number of errors, or measured speed in performing a task. Thus the dependent variables are the measured changes in pupil peroformance attributable to the influence of the independent variable. A difference between subjects that cannot be controlled but can only be selected. These are called subject variables. Examples of subject variables are poverty and the sex, age or intelligence quotient of a person. These independent variables cannot be controlled by the researcher. There are two types of independent variables: treatment and organismic or attribute variables.

Treatment variables are those factors that the experimenter manipulates and to which he or she assigns subjects. Attribute variables are those characteristics that cannot be altered by the experimenter. Such independent variables as age, sex, race, and intelligence level have already been determined, but the experimenter can decide to include them or remove them as variables to be studied. The question of whether 8-years old girls show greater reading achievement than 8-years old boys in an example of the use of an organismic variable, sex. The teaching procedure is the same for both groups so there is no treatment independent variable.

Confounded Variables

Confounded variables are one whose effect cannot be separated from the supposed independent variable.

Confounding variables are those aspects of a study or sample that might influence the dependent variable and whose effect may be confused with the effect of the independent variable. Confounding variables are of two types: Intervening and extraneous variables.

(a) Intervening Variables

In many types of behavioural research the relationship between the independent and dependent variables is not a simple one of stimulus to response. Certain variables which cannot be controlled or measured directly may have an important effect upon the outcome. These modifying variables intervene between the cause and the effect.

In a classroom language experiment a researcher is interested in determining the effect of immediate reinforcement upon learning the parts of speech. He or she suspects that certain factors or variables, other than the one being studied, immediate reinforcement, may be influencing the results, even though they cannot be observed directly. These factors, anxiety, fatigue, motivation, for example, may be intervening variables. They are difficult to define in operational, observable, terms, but they cannot be ignored.

(b) Extraneous Variables

Extraneous variables are those uncontrolled variables that may have a significant influence upon the results of a study. Many research conclusions are questionable because of the influence of these extraneous variables.

Extraneous variables are independent variables that have not been controlled. Some of the variables that could have an effect on the learning student in a classroom situation. There are many possible extraneous variables that might have an effect on student learning here. The personality of the teachers involving is one possibility. The intelligence level of students is another. Time of day the classes taught, nature of the subject taught, textbook used, type of learning activities, the teacher and teaching methods—all are possible for other variables that could affect learning. Such variables would probably be extraneous variables in this study.

Qualitative and Categories Variables

A quantitative variable is one that varies in amount, whereas a categorical variable varies in kind. Examples of quantitative variables would be speed of response and loudness. College major and gender would be categorical variables.

Quantitative variables can often (but not always) be subdivided into smaller and smaller units. "Length", for example, can be measured in miles, yards, feet, inches or in whatever subdivision of an inch is needed. Categorical variables do not vary in degree, amount, or quantity but are qualitatively different. Examples include eye colour, gender, religious preference, occupation, position on a base ball team, and most kinds of research "treatments" or "methods". For example, if a researcher wished to compare computerized and non-computerized classrooms, the variable involved would be the presence or absence of computers. This is a categorical variable—a classroom is either one or other-either computerized or non computerized, not some where on a continuum between being computerized and not being computerized. All members within each category of this variable are considered the same.

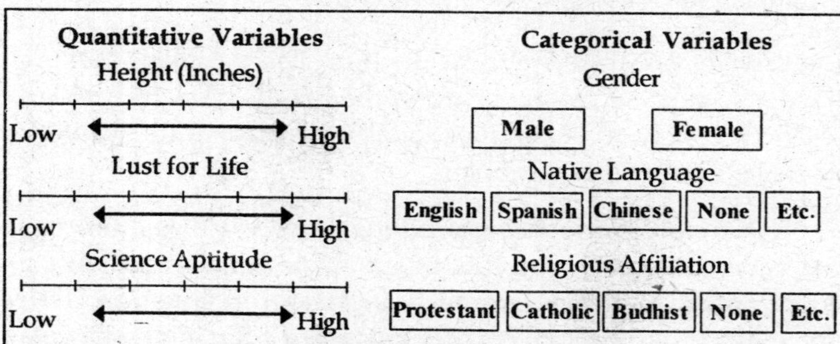

Figure 11.1: Illustration of Quantitative Compared with Categorical Variables

Categorical variables are:

1. Type of automobile owened
2. Ethnicity

3. Gender

Quantitative variables are:

1. Learning ability
2. Cohesiveness
3. Heart beat rate

Most research in education studies the relationship between either (1) two (or more) quantitative variables, (2) one categorical and one quantitative variable, or (3) two or more categorical variables. Here are some examples of each:

1. *Two Quantitative Variables*
   - Age and amount of interest in school
   - Reading achievement and Mathematics achievement
   - Classroom humanism and student motivation
   - Amount of time watching television and aggressiveness of behaviour.
2. *One Categorical and One Quantitative Variables*
   - Method used to teach reading and reaching achievement
   - Counseling approach and level of anxiety
   - Nationality and liking for school
   - Student gender and amount of praise given by teachers.
3. *Two Categorical Variables*
   - Ethnicity and father's occupation
   - Gender of teacher and subject taught
   - Administrative style and college major
   - Religious affiliation and political party membership.

Continuous and Discrete Variables

Some quantitative variables can take any value on a continuum. They are called continuous variables because they are not limited to a certain number of values, such as whole numbers, or to discrete bins.

Discrete variables is one that falls into separate bins with no intermediate values possible. The number of marriages contracted, murders committed, or books written are all discrete variables.

Although a variable may be continuous its measurement is often discontinuous. Although height is a continuous variable, generally measure it to the nearest inch. Similarly, knowledge of psychological research methods may be a continuous variables, but it is often measured by the number of items correct on a test, a discontinuous measure. This does not make knowledge is a discrete variable because it would be possible in principle to measure knowledge as finely as one wished.

Continuous variable are commonly measured in a discontinuous fashion, it is necessary to distinguish the real limits of a measure from the apparent limits. The point indicated by a number is called apparent limits. For example, a score 1, 2, or some whole number.

The interval defined by the number plus or minus half the distance to the next number is called real limits.

For example, 0.5 to 1.5, 1.5 to 2.5 and so on.

Manipulated and Outcome Variables

There are two or more experimental conditions, they create a variable, for example, that a researcher decided to investigate the effect of different amounts of reinforcement on reading achievement and systematically assigns students to three different groups. One group is praised continuously every day during their reading session. The second group is told simply to "keep up the good work." While the third group is told nothing at all. The researcher, in effect, manipulates the conditions in the experiment, thereby creating the variable "amount of reinforcement." Whenever experimental conditions are set up by a researcher one or more variables are created. Such variables are called *experimental variables* or *manipulated variable* or *treatment variables*.

In an experiment outcomes vary for different people, in different situations and under different conditions, they are often called outcome variables. All the following can be example of outcome variables.

- The amount of uneasiness that applicants for a position express in an interview.
- How anxious students are before an examination.
- Neatness.
- The "Openness" of a classroom.
- How disruptive students are in a history class.
- The ability of people to express themselves in writing.
- Fluency in a foreign language.
- Teacher-student rapport.

Experimental Group

The experimental group is exposed to influence of the factor under consideration observations are then made to determine what differences appears or what change or modifications occurs is the experimental as contrasted with control group.

Control Group

Control group is not exposed to the influence of the factor under consideration. A control group receives nothing additional as a result of two study.

REFERENCES

1. Young, P. *Scientific Social Surveys and Research.*
2. Cohein, L. and Manian, L. (1994). *Research Methods in Education.* New York: Routledge.
3. Burney, M., Donald, H. (2001). *Research Methods*. Australia: Wordsworth.

12

Hypotheses

Introduction

Once the selection and definition of the problem have been accomplished, the derivation of hypothesis is the most important step in a research process. Etymologically the term, hypothesis is made up of two words 'hypo' and 'thesis' which means less than or less certain than a thesis.

Hypothesis is a reasonable guess or statement based upon the available evidence, which the researcher seeks to prove through the study.

The hypothesis is a powerful tool in research process to achieve dependable knowledge. It help the researcher to relate theory to observation and observation to theory. Hypothesis is formulated only as the suggested solution to the problem, with the objective that the ensuring study may lead either to into rejection or to its retention. They enable the researcher to locate and identify the variables involved in the study and suggest methodological procedures that are to be employed. From the research scholar's point of view, the hypothesis may be conveniently considered as a tentative or working assumption and the theory as the surviving or final hypothesis which is most defensibly supported by all the evidence.

Importance of the Hypotheses

Hypotheses are very important in studies which aim to make

predictions about some outcome. It is of atmost importance in researches involving experiments. In the historical or descriptive research, the researcher is investigating the history of a city, or nation, or the happening of an event etc. and so may not have a basis for making a prediction of results. A hypothesis, therefore, may not be required in such fact finding studies.

A. Hypotheses help in the extension of knowledge in an area. It provide tentative explanations of facts and phenomena and can be tested and validated and it lead to generalization.

B. Hypotheses provide the researcher with rational statements, consisting of elements expressed in a logical order of relationships which seek to describe or to explain conditions or events, that have not yet been confirmed by facts. And the hypotheses help the researcher to relate logically known facts to intelligent guesses about unknown conditions.

C. Hypotheses provide direction to the research. They represent specific objectives and thus help the researcher to determine the type of data needed to test the preposition. The hypotheses tell the researcher specifically what he needed to do and find out in his study. They help in the selection of relevant facts and variables that the researcher needs in his study. Hypotheses provide a basis for selecting the sample and the research procedures to be uses in the study and the statistical techniques needed in the analysis.

D. The hypothesis enable the researcher to relate logically known facts to unknown conditions.

E. The hypotheses help the researcher to limit his study in scope of the hypotheses formulated and so that it does not become broad or unwieldy.

F. Hypotheses provide the bases for reporting the conclusions of the study. The researcher will find it very convenient to test each hypothesis separately and state the conclusion that are relevant to each.

Formulation of the Hypotheses

Hypotheses are guesses or tentative generalization, but these guesses are not merely accidents. Collection of factual information above does not lead to successful formulation of hypotheses. Hypotheses are the product of considerable speculation and imaginative guess work. They are based partially conceptual. Following are the certain necessary conditions that are needed for their formulation.

A. Richness of Background Knowledge

A researcher may deduce hypotheses inductively after making observations of behaviour, noticing trends or probable relationships. Background knowledge, however, is essential for perceiving relationships among the variables and to determine what findings other researchers have reported on the problem under study. Relevant to a particular problem various researchers may have different hypotheses but the soundness of the hypotheses will depend upon the quantum of knowledge that one possess of the area of investigation.

B. Versatility of Intellect

Hypotheses are also derived through deductive reasoning from a theory. Such hypotheses are called deductive hypotheses. A researcher starts his study after selecting a theory the researcher proceeds to deduce a hypotheses from this theory through symbolic logic or mathematics. This is possible only when the researcher has a versatile intellect and can make use of it for restructuring his experiences.

C. Analogy and Other Practices

Analogy will lead the researcher to clues that he might find useful in the formulation of hypotheses and for finding solutions to problems. The researcher however, should use analogies with caution as they are not full proof tool for finding solutions to problems.

D. Consultation

Conversations and consultations with colleagues and experts from different fields are helpful in formulating significant hypotheses.

Criteria of Usable Hypotheses

While formulating a hypotheses the researcher should take atmost care. Following are the suggested criteria to which a hypotheses should conform.

A. Hypotheses should be clearly and precisely stated. The clear statement of hypotheses generally involves concise technical language and definition of terms that are better defined than those in common language.

B. Hypotheses should be testable or verifiable and it is necessary to draw conclusions.

C. Hypotheses should state the expected relationship between variables implicitly.

D. Hypotheses should be limited scope. Hypotheses of global significance are not usable because they are not specific and simple for testing and drawing conclusions.

E. Hypotheses should be consistent with most known facts. It should not be inconsistent with a substantial body of established facts. They should be grounded in the well established theories and laws.

F. Hypotheses should be stated as far as possible in simple terms. It makes their meaning clear to others, but also helps in their testability.

G. The hypotheses selected should be amendable to testing within a reasonable time.

Advantages of Hypotheses

A. A hypotheses helps in deep thinking of possible outcomes.

B. More sophisticated understanding is possible through forming hypotheses.

C. Researcher are not only answering to the hypothesis but also they are attempting to build a body of knowledge. So hypotheses helps in developing new knowledge.

D. Formulating hypotheses has a philosophical basis and it helps in continuous proving of the basis hypotheses or facts.

E. When one form hypotheses, the relationship is automatically formed. If not the researcher has to form it.

Disadvantages of Hypotheses

A. Hypotheses may lead to bias, conscious or unconscious, of the researcher. i.e., they may manipulate the data and procedure in such a way to get desired outcome, for providing the stated hypotheses. But it is assumed to be intellectually honest.

B. A hypotheses may prevent the researcher from noticing the other relevant phenomena other than the hypotheses variables.

Statement of Hypotheses

Important characteristics of many research is that they suggest a relationship of some sort to be investigated. It is very important since the descriptive type question will answer only to what is happened and not why happened. The relationship may be either existing (real) or not existing (unreal).

After review of literature researchers write a hypothesis. While writing or stating a hypothesis the researcher has to care following things.

A. Are any assumptions advanced with respect to the hypothesis or question? If so, are they explicit (they should be), or are they implicit?

B. Are hypotheses consistent with theory and known facts? Are they testable? Do they provide a suggested answer to the problem?

C. Are all terms adequately defined in operational fashion?

All questions can't be a research problem. In conventional sense, a problem is a set of conditions needing discussion, a decision, a solution or information. A research problem implies the possibility of empirical investigation—that is data collection and analysis.

Classification of Stating Hypotheses or Types of Hypotheses

We can classify or state a research hypothesis in many ways. Or there are many ways in stating a hypothesis.

A. Directional and Non-directional Hypotheses

(i) Directional Hypothesis

A hypothesis in which the specific direction (such as higher, lower, more than or less than, or positive or negative) that a researcher expected to emerge in a relationship; is indicted.

For example, Adolescent boys with high IQ will exhibit low anxiety than adolescent boys with low IQ.

(ii) Non-directional Hypotheses

If the researcher suspects that a relationship exists, but has no basis for predicting the direction of relationship and so, the researcher do not make a specific direction for the hypothesis and such hypotheses are called non-directional hypotheses.

For example, There is a difference in the anxiety level of adolescent girls of high IQ and low IQ.

B. Declarative Hypotheses

When the researcher makes a positive statement about the outcome of the study the hypotheses takes the declarative form. In such a statement of hypothesis, the researcher makes a prediction based on his theoretical formulation of what should happen if the explanations of the behaviour he has given in his theory are correct.

For example, The academic achievement of extroverts is significantly higher than that of the introverts.

C. Null or Statistical or Testing Hypothesis

A null hypothesis makes a statement that no relationship exists. It is often termed as statistical hypothesis since the null hypothesis can be tested statistically. In a research, if the hypothesis is stated as declarative it can be tested statistically only by converting it into null form. So the null hypothesis is also called as testing hypothesis. A null hypothesis challenges the assertion of a declarative and denies it altogether. It is pointed out that null hypothesis should not be used as an alternative to the declarative hypothesis but should be used in combination with it for statistical purpose.

For example, There is no significant difference between the academic achievement of students who are athletes and that of non-athletes.

D. Question Form Hypothesis

In question form hypothesis a question is asked to what the outcome will be instead setting what outcome is expected. The researcher than use question form hypothesis when he experiences some difficulty in predicting the outcome of the study and stating the hypothesis in declarative form. But it must be noted that the question form is less powerful than the declarative or null form as a tool for obtaining valid information.

For example, "Will there any significant difference between the academic achievement of students who are athletes and that of non-athletes?

E. Significant Hypothesis

There may be more than one possible hypothesis suggested by a research question. Some of them are more significant than others and they are called significant hypothesis. Significant here means which lead to more useful knowledge.

Conclusion

It is very important for the researcher to formulate hypothesis before data are gathered. This is necessary for an objective and unbiased study.

The formulation of the research hypothesis typically is determined by the implication of the related literature and the deductive logic of the problem under investigation. Formulation of research hypothesis gives the researcher with the direction to the data gathering procedure. It is in the light of hypothesis that he relevance of data collected is judged.

REFERENCES

1. Kubiszyn, T. and Borich, G. (1993). *Educational Testing and Measurement Classroom Application and Practice*. New York: Harper Collins College Publishers.
2. Gupta, S. (1993). *Research Methodology and Statistical Techniques*. New Delhi: Deep and Deep Publications.
3. Best, J.W. and Khan, J.V. *Research in Education*.
4. Frankel, J.R. and Wallen, N.E. *How to Design and Evaluate Research in Education*, McGraw Hill.

13
Sampling

Introduction

Sampling may be defined as the selection of some part of an aggregate or totality on the basis of which a judgement or inference about the aggregate or totality is made. In other words, it is the process of obtaining information about an entire population by examining only a part of it. In most of the research work and surveys, the usual approach happens to be to make generalizations or to draw inferences based on samples are taken. The researcher quite often selects only a few items from the universe for his study purposes. All this is done on the assumption that the sample data will enable him to estimate the population parameters. The items so selected constitute what is technically called a sample, their selection process or technique is called sample design and the survey conducted on the basis of sample is described as sample survey. Sample should be truly representative of population characteristics with out any bias so that it may result in valid and reliable conclusions. Bloomers and Lindquist observed, "A large majority of the research studies in education and psychology, or for that matter, in many other fields, are of a type known as sampling studies. In such studies, measurements or observations are made of a limited number or sample of individuals or objects in order that generalizations or inferences may be drawn about still larger groups or populations of the individuals or objects that these samples are supposed to represent."

Need for Sampling

Sampling is used in practice for a variety of reasons such as:

1. Sampling can save time and money.
2. Sampling may enable more accurate measurements, for a sample study is generally conducted by trained and experienced investigators.
3. Sampling remains the only way when population contains infinitely many members.
4. Sampling remains the only choice when a test involves the destruction of the item under study.
5. Sampling usually enables to estimate the sampling errors and, thus, assists in obtaining information concerning some characteristic of the population.

Some Important Definitions of Related Terms

Population

The aggregate or totality of objects or individuals regarding which inferences are to be made in a sampling study.

Sample

A sample is a small proportion of a population selected for observation and analysis.

Sampling

It is the process of selecting a sample from the population. For this purpose, the population is divided into a number of parts called sampling units.

Parameter

A parameter is a population fact which depends upon or is a function of the scores for all the population units. It is the population value representing any trait or characteristic of the population as a whole.

Statistics

A statistic is a sample fact which depends upon the scores of the particular sampling units comprising a sample. It is the sample value representing any trait or characteristic of the members of the sampling.

Sampling Error

Sampling error is simply the difference between the value of parameter and that of corresponding statistic or the difference between population value and sample value.

Sampling Error = Frame error + chance error + response error

Sampling Distribution

The sampling distribution is the relative frequency distribution of an infinity of determinations of the value of this statistic. Each determination is based on a separate sample of the same size and selected independently by the same prescribed procedure from the same population.

Sampling Bias

If the mean of the sampling distribution of a statistic coincides with or equals that of the corresponding parameter it is said to be unbiased. If, on the other hand, the mean of its sampling distribution does not coincide with the parameter, it is said to be biased.

Standard Error

The standard error of any statistic is the standard deviation of its sampling distribution.

Bases of Sampling

The choice of the sample as representative of the whole group is based upon the following assumptions:

1. *Homogeneity Among Complexity*: Fundamentally speaking, the students are similar in many respects so that a study of some of them will throw significant

light upon the whole group. Beneath the diversity and complexity of the nature of students, there is an underlying similarity and homogeneity.

2. *Possibility of Representative Selection*: It has been observed that if a certain number of units are selected from a population or universe on purely random basis, each unit has an equal opportunity of being included in the sample as the representative of the whole group.

3. *Absolute/cent per cent Accuracy not Essential:* In large scale studies, the research workers have to depend upon averages and estimates which are considered as fairly significant in an enquiry. The results of sampling studies turn out to be fairly accurate to permit valid generalizations.

Characteristics of a Good Sample

1. A good sample reproduces the characteristics of the population with the greatest possible accuracy, of course within restrictions imposed by its size.

2. A sample should be free from error due to bias or due to deliberate selection of the unit of sample.

3. A good sample should be free from random sampling error.

4. It should be selected by a procedure where there is no connection between the method of selection and the characteristics under consideration.

5. It should be free from in complete coverage of the units selected for study, i.e., it should not ignore the failures in the sample in responding to the study.

6. Properly selected small samples may be relatively much more reliable than large samples poorly selected.

7. A good sample is adequate in size so that it can become really reliable.

8. Only such units should be included in the sample, which, as far as possible, are independent.

9. In the selection of a good sample, measurable or known probability sample techniques are used.

Uses of Sampling

1. A large population can be satisfactorily covering.

2. When the data are unlimited, this method becomes very handy.

3. Sampling is very useful when the units are relatively homogenous.

4. Sampling inevitable when absolute accuracy is not required.

5. Sampling makes intensive study possible when the number of individuals to be studied in manageable.

Steps in Sampling Procedure

W.C. Cochran has suggested the following principle steps in the sampling procedure.

1. Formulation of the clear statement of the objectives of the study.

2. Clear demarcation and definition of the population to be sampled.

3. Use of appropriate tools and devices of measurement.

4. No. overlapping in the choice of a sampling unit.

5. Selection of adequate size of the samples.

6. Supervision of the work.

7. Collection of samples.

8. Tabulation and analysis of samples.

9. Dissemination of the information obtained.

Advantages of Sampling

1. Reduced cost—economical.
2. Greater spead—less time consuming.
3. Greater scope—simplifying, collection, tabulation etc.
4. Greater accuracy.
5. Convenient organization.
6. Exhaustive and Intensive data.
7. Suitable in limited resources.
8. Better rapport between investigator and respondents.

Disadvantages of Sampling

1. Sampling may involve biased selection of respondents on the part of the research worker.
2. Selection of a truly representative sample is very difficult. A large number of factors stand in the way of selecting good samples.
3. Sampling method needs a specialized knowledge and in its absence, the investigator may commit serious mistakes.
4. The subjects of the sample may be widely dispersed.
5. It is not suitable where a higher standard of accuracy is expected.
6. Sometime the universe/population is so small or so heterogeneous that it is not possible to derive a representative sample. In such a situation census study is the only alternative.
7. Possibilities of bias and prejudices.

Size of the Sample

According to Parten—"An optimum sample in survey is one which fulfils the requirements of efficiency, representativeness, reliability and flexibility. The sample should be small enough to avoid, unnecessary expenses and larger enough to avoid intolerable sampling error."

Large Samples

Large samples are desirable and often essential under these conditions:

1. *Presence of many uncontrolled variables:* When it is not possible for the research worker to control some of the important variables that could have an effect upon the research findings. It is advisable to employ large random samples. This would develop more confidence in the research workers and his findings become more reliable.

2. *Possibility of small differences:* In many educational groups research problems where only small differences on the dependent variables are expected, it is desirable to use large samples.

3. *When Groups must be broken into subgroups:* When groups are analyzed on the basis of rural or urban area, boys and girls, income status of the family etc., a large number of cases should be selected.

4. *When the population is not homogenous on the variables being studied:* If every person in the population were exactly alike in the variable studied, a sample of one would be adequate. As the population becomes highly heterogeneous, large sample must be used.

Small Samples

Small samples are more appropriate in the following types of cases:

(a) Role-playing studies

(b) Depth interviews

(c) Projective measures

Size of the Sample

Apart from the representativeness of the sample another important issue is the size of the sample. There can be no blanket answer for that. Size of the sample depends on the nature of the study, size of the population, sampling design, parameters used and estimated, range of unreliability and an estimate of dispersion of the characteristic under investigation. As an illustration, suppose the researcher decides,

(i) to use 95 per cent level of confidence

(ii) to accept 1 per cent error, which means that the sample means does not differ from the population mean by more than ½ per cent.

He has found the Standard Deviation of his group to be 10. The sample size (N) can be calculated from the formula S.E. m = S.D √N. We know that the value of Z for 95 per cent confidence level is 1.96.

$$\therefore 1.96 \text{ S.E.m} = \frac{1}{2} \text{ or } 1.96 \times \text{S.D.} = \sqrt{N} \times \frac{1}{2}$$

$$\text{or } N = 4 \times (1.96)^2 \times (\text{S.D})^2$$

$$= 4 \times 3.8416 \times 100 = 4 \times 384 = 1536$$

Thus 1536 cases should be taken in this sample. We can calculate the size of the sample for 96 per cent confidence level and 1 per cent error. In this case Z-value is 2.58.

$$\therefore 2.58 \frac{SD}{\sqrt{N}} = 1$$

$$\text{or } \sqrt{N} = 1 \times 2.58 \times \text{S.D.}$$

$$\text{or } N = 1 \times (2.58)^2 \times 100$$

$$= 1 \times 6.6564 \times 100$$

$$= 1 \times 665.64 = 665.64$$

Therefore the adequate size of the sample is 666.

Factors Determining the Size of the Sample

1. Nature of the Study.

2. Nature of the Universe.
3. Number of the Classes.
4. Practical considerations and accuracy.
5. Questionnaire and Schedule and nature of the cases to be contacted.
6. Types and nature of the sampling.

Representative Character of the Sample

1. The size of the sample should not be too small and the selection should not be done purposeless.
2. Imperfect stratification and absence of an incomplete source list.
3. Lack of source list or availability of incomplete source list makes the samples biased.
4. Loss of cases replacement of cases.
5. Field workers and their convenience.
6. Method of drawing samples and nature of phenomenon.

Reliability of the Sampling—How it Tested?

1. Size of the sample—adequate.
2. By testing the representativeness of the sample.
3. By drawing a parallel sampling.
4. By testing the homogeneity of the samples.
5. Through comparison of the measurement of the sample with those of the universe.
6. Through unbiased selection.
7. By taking a sub-sample from a main sample.

...tion of a Sample

... should be a sample selected?

1. *Clear-cut definition of the universe*: The whole population out of which the samples are selected, in the technical phraseology of research is known as 'Universe'. The definition of the universe is not a very easy task. It done very cautiously. For the convenience of the definition, the universe may be categorized under following four heads.
   - *(a)* Definite universe
   - *(b)* Indefinite universe
   - *(c)* Real universe
   - *(d)* Hypothetical universe
2. *Decision about the units of the sample or sampling units*: Parton observed, "Surveyors have fallen into the error of thinking that as long as they are dealing with human population the individual persons are the sampling unit. Actually, however relatively few of studies have used people as a sampling units."

Types of Sampling Units

- Geographical Units
- Structural Units
- Social Group
- Individual

Different Methods of Sampling

Bloomers and Lindquist have said—"In general sampling schemes may be classified according to two types":

1. Those in which sample elements are automatically selected by some schteme under which a particular sample of a given size from a specified population has some known probability of being selected, and
2. Those in which the sample elements are arbitrarily selected by the sampler because in his judgement the

elements thus chosen will most effectively represent the population.

Probability and Non-Probability Sampling

Hence according to them, there are two chief methods of sampling:

1. The probability sampling, and
2. The judgement sampling.

In non-probability sampling, the units are selected at the discretion of the researcher. Such samples used human judgement in selecting units and have no theoretical basis for estimating population characteristics. If the researcher is to select a sample of 200 students, he may exercise his own judgement based on experience for including a given students in the sample. The sample so selected is called a judgement or purposive sample. Such a sample is arbitrarily selected because there is good evidence that it is a representative of the total population. The evidence is always based on experience. For example, in a study of delinquency, the researcher on the basis of his past experience, selects certain areas that have shown higher rate of delinquent acts in the past.

Quota or Chunk sample, incidental or volunteer sampling are the examples of non-probability sampling. The non-probability sampling methods are very convenient in the situations when the sample to be selected is very small and the researcher wants to get some idea of the population characteristics in a short time. Such samples are used in the situations where the researcher does not want a representative sample but to gain insight into the problem by selecting only informed persons who can provide him the maximum degree of insight into his problem with comprehensive information.

The following are some limitations in the use of non-probability sampling methods:

1. No confidence can be placed in the data obtained from such samples and results thus obtained cannot be

generalized for the entire population. Generalizations beyond any sample can be made safely only when it represents the population in every significant respect.

2. The selective sampling based on convenience affects the variance within groups as well as between groups and so sampling error of such samples cannot be determined.
3. Sometimes such samples are based on an obsolete frame which does not adequately cover the population.
4. Non-probability samples depend exclusively on uncontrolled factors and researcher's insight, and there is no statistical method to determine the margin of sampling errors.

Probability Sampling

In probability sampling, the units of the population are not selected at the discretion of the researcher, but by means of certain procedures which ensure that every unit of a population has one fixed probability of being included in the sample. Such a method is also called random sampling.

According to Good (1996, p. 217) probability samples have the following characteristics.

1. Each unit in the sample has some known probability of entering the sample.
2. Weights appropriate to the probabilities are used in the analysis of sample.
3. The process of sampling is automatic in one or more steps of selection of units in the sample.

In probability sampling, a researcher designs the sample in a way that ensures that each unity in the population has a fair chance of being selected and he can find out the numerical value of that chance. With such samples, the researcher may be able to:

(i) Know the size of the sample needed to achieve any desired level of accuracy.

(ii) Specify the chance of each unit being selected.

(iii) Estimate the magnitude of error due to sampling.

(iv) Determine the levels of confidence.

There are different methods of selecting a probability sample, all of which have their own advantages and limitations.

1. Simple and unrestricted sampling
2. Stratified Random Sampling
3. Systematic Sampling
4. Cluster and Multi-stage sampling

Various Classifications of Sampling Methods

1. The simple random sampling
2. Systematic sampling
3. Stratified sampling
4. Purposive sampling
5. Quota sampling
6. Cluster sampling
7. Double sampling
8. Judgement sampling
9. Sequential sampling
10. Incidental sampling
11. Convenience sampling
12. Self selected sampling

1. Random Sampling

Parten; "Random sampling is the form applied when the methods of selection assure each individual or element in universe an equal chance of being chosen'. Random sampling is not the same as chance selection. In random sampling population is numbered from 1 to N and a series of numbers is drawn either by means of a table of random numbers (These are many tables available) and we can begin at any point on any page and choose the required number of units or by placing the numbers in a bowl, mixing them thoroughly and drawing N numbers in succession. Tables of random numbers have been prepared by Fisher, and Yates, Tippet, Kendall Balington-Smith. Random sampling is neither arbitrary nor careless and nor haphazard.

Chief Methods of Drawing Random Sample

1. Lottery method
2. Tippet's numbers method
3. Selecting from sequential list
4. Grid System

1. *Lottery Method*: In this method, a lottery is drawn by writing the numbers or the names of various units and putting them in a container. They are thoroughly mixed and certain numbers are picked up from the container, and those which we picked up are 'taken up for sampling'.

2. *Tippett's Numbers Method:* It was evolved by L.H.C. Tippet who constructed a list of 10,4000 four digit numbers written at random on every page. For example, if 50 persons are to be selected for study out of the total number of 500, then we can open any page of Tippet's numbers and select first 50 that are below 500 and take them up for study. On the basis of the experiments carried out through this technique, it has been found that the results that are drawn on the basis of this method of random sampling, are quite reliable.

3. *Selection from Sequential List:* In this method, the names are arranged serially according to a particular order. The order may be alphabetical, geographical or only

school, students enrolled in a particular class, members of a club, children of an orphanage or a reformatory etc. The investigator uses these readily available units because he is unable to employ more acceptable sampling methods. The number and conditions of the study. This method may be quite acceptable for certain action research projects which do not require generalizations concerning any population other than the sample group used. Non-parametric statistics may be used in the analysis of results. Such groups are but poor samples of any definable population and adequate generalizations can hardly be based upon such data.

11. Convenience Sampling

It is generally known as careless, un-systematic accidental or opportunistic sampling. The sample is selected according to the convenience of the sample. He selects certain units convenient to him. No pre-planning is necessary for the selection of items. The convenience may be in respect of availability of source list, accessibility of the units, etc. Although this method is most unscientific, yet quite a large number of samples are of this very type.

(a) Convenience sampling may be used in any one or more of these cases when as the universe is not clearly defined.

(b) Sampling unit is not clear, and

(c) A complete source list is not available.

12. Self Selected Sample

Sometimes the units of the sample are not actually selected by the investigator, the people offer themselves for selection. They opt to be included or not to be included in the study. Suppose, for example, an enquiry has to be made about the people's liking for a particular radio programme, and an announcement and this effect is made on the radio asking the people to volunteer themselves to participate in the study. Thus people come forward on their own to act as subjects of the study. In

Non Random Sampling Methods

Population

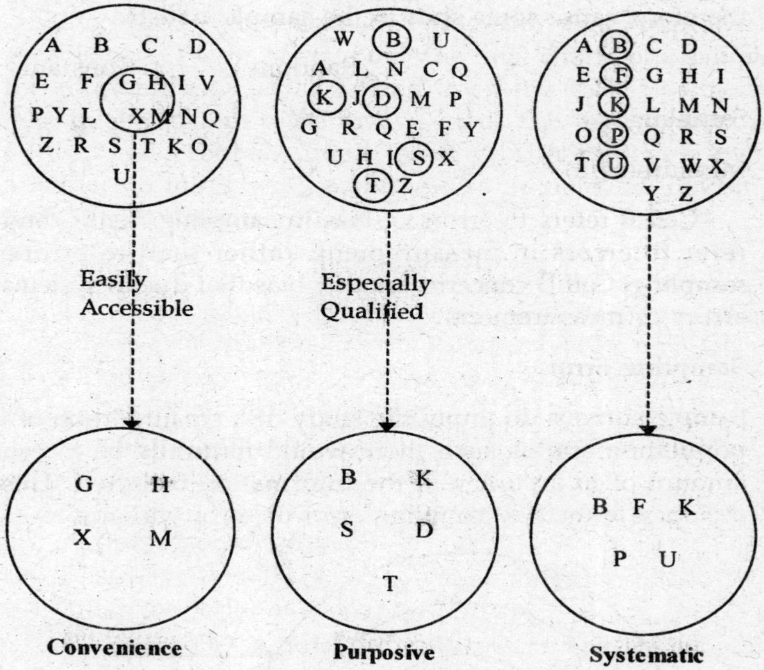

Samples

Figure 13.2: Non-Random Sampling Method

such a case the units are not specifically fixed. Those who care to respond to the announcement from the part of the sample.

Errors in Sampling

Classification of Sampling Errors

Sample data are not representative, can suffer from errors of a random and/or a systematic nature. These errors can be classified further as errors of sampling and/or measurement providing a four-way classification. Cell 'A' refers to the unavoidable errors that occur whenever sampling is done. If

14

Measures of Central Tendency

Computation of Arithmetic Mean, Median and Mode, Merits and Demerits of Different Measures

Measures of central tendency are most common with the statisticians because these measures help them to reduce the complexity of data and made it comparable. We cannot remember the whole set of data and the analysis of such data is impossible. So in order to reduce the complexity and make the data comparable, we sort to averaging. This average must be representative of the whole data. Average is the value of the variable round which they centre or is generally located in the middle of the distribution.

Measures of Central Tendency

1. Arithmetic Mean

The most popular measure for representing the entire data is the arithmetic mean (AM). A.M. of a set of observations is a figure (numerical value) obtained by dividing the total of all the observations by their number, Arithmetic mean can be either;

(i) Simple arithmetic mean

or

(ii) Weighted arithmetic mean

Calculation of Simple Arithmetic Mean

Method I

If we represent the individual values of the variable X by x_1, x_2, x_n (n = number of observations). We shall denote by ($\bar{x}$, read as × bar) the A.M. of the variable x. also the symbol Σx (read as summation x) denotes the sum of x values, i.e.,

$\Sigma x = X_1 + X_2 + \ldots\ldots + X_n$. Then according to the definition

$$X = \frac{X1 + X2 + \ldots\ldots + Xn}{n} = \frac{\Sigma x}{n}$$

Illustration: The following are the weights of 10 students of class.

Sl. No.	1	2	3	4	5	6	7	8	9	10
Weight in Kg's	45	48	50	60	55	46	50	58	62	46

Solution: Calculation of Arithmetic Mean:

$$\text{A.M. } \overline{X} = \frac{45 + 48 + 50 + 60 + 55 + 46 + 50 + 58 + 62 + 46}{10}$$

$$= \frac{520}{10} = 52 \text{ kg.}$$

Method II

By taking the deviation of individual observations from an arbitrary value, the arithmetic mean can be calculated by using the formula,

$\overline{X} = A + \frac{\Sigma d}{n}$, where 'A' denotes the arbitrary value, 'Σd' the sum of deviations and 'n' the number of observations. For above problem if we choose A = 50 then deviations are:

$d = -5, -2, 0, +10, +5, -4, 0, +8, +12, -4; \Sigma d = 20$

and $\therefore \overline{X} = 50 + \frac{20}{10} = 50 + 2 = 52$

frequency corresponding to a variable value is the sum of frequencies of the value up to the given value.

Steps for Calculating the Median are,

(i) Write a column of cumulative frequency in addition to given columns of variable and frequency 'f'.

(ii) Calculate the value of $\frac{N+1}{2}$ where N = total number of observations.

Merits and Demerits of Median

The median is not affected by extreme scores, it represents central tendency better than the mean when distributions are skewed. In skewed distributions the near is 'pulled' towards the extremes, so that in some cases it may give a falsely high or falsely low estimate of central tendency.

Since the median, on other hand, is the score above and below which half the scores lie, it always indicates the centre of the distribution.

The median be considered when skewed distribution are involved. Too often, however, only the average or mean is reported when statistics are presented, without regard for the shape of the distribution.

The Mode

The observation that occurs most frequently in the set of observations is called the mode. In many situations arithmetic mean and median fail to reveal the true characteristics of the data.

Calculation of Mode for Individual Observations

For finding mode of a given set of observations, we shall count the number of times the various values repeat themselves. The value of the observation occurring the maximum number of times is called the mode.